AF594747

SEA WITCH

PHOTOGRAPHS, POEMS AND FORGET-ME-NOTS FROM A MAINER GROWING UP

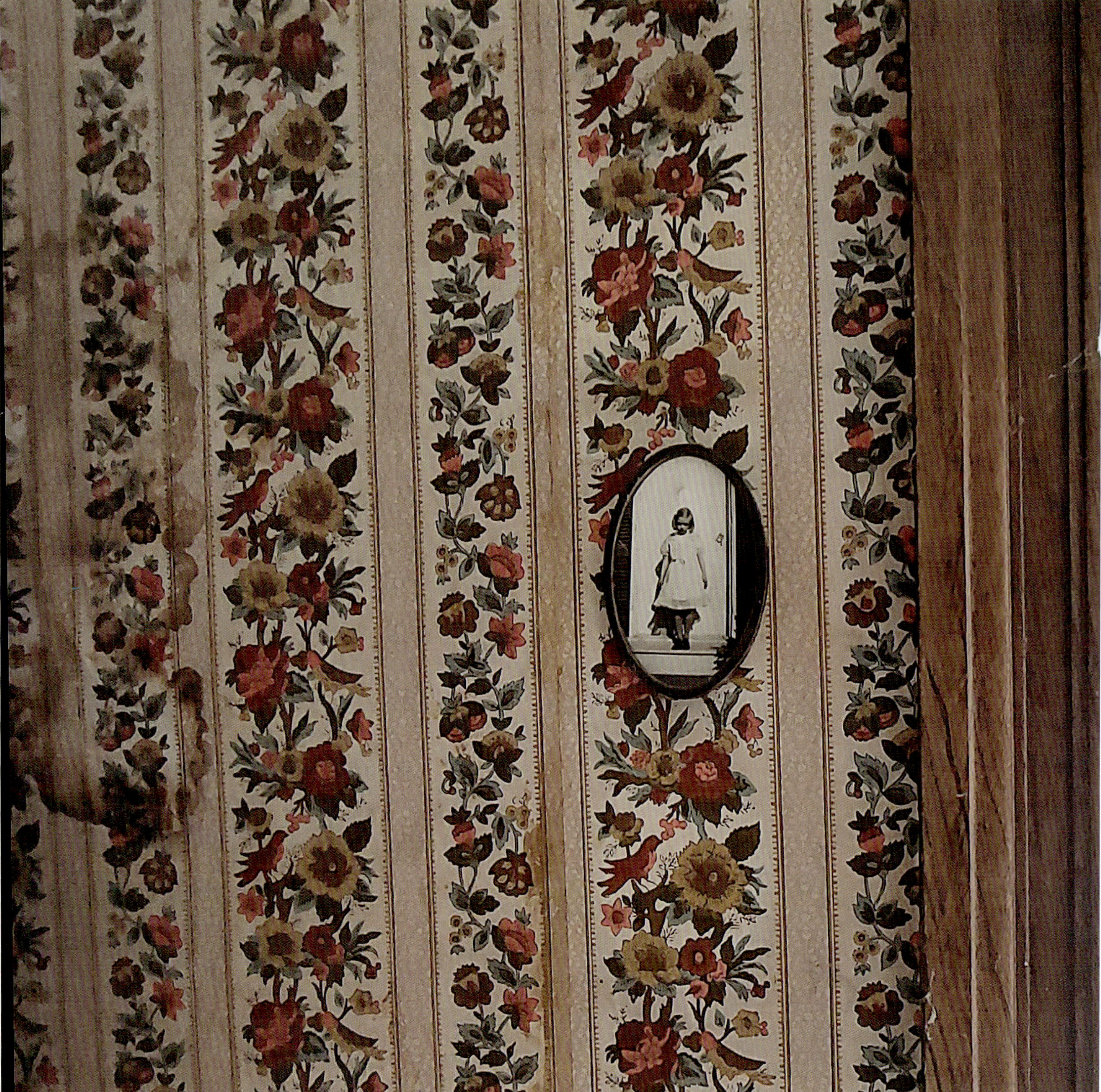

SEA WITCH

PHOTOGRAPHS, POEMS AND FORGET-ME-NOTS FROM A MAINER GROWING UP

KRISTIE BILLINGS

Sea Witch

Photographs, Poems and Forget-Me-Nots
from a Mainer Growing Up

Copyright © 2023
All rights are reserved.
No part of this book may be reproduced or transmitted in any form
by any means, electronic or mechanical, including photocopying and recording,
or by any information storage or retrieval system, without written permission from
Seapoint Books + Media LLC
PO Box 21, Brooklin, ME 04616
seapointbooks.com

Design and composition by Jennifer Muller Design
jennifermullerdesign.com

Printed by Printworks Global Ltd., London & Hong Kong

First Edition

ISBN: 979-8-9872084-2-7

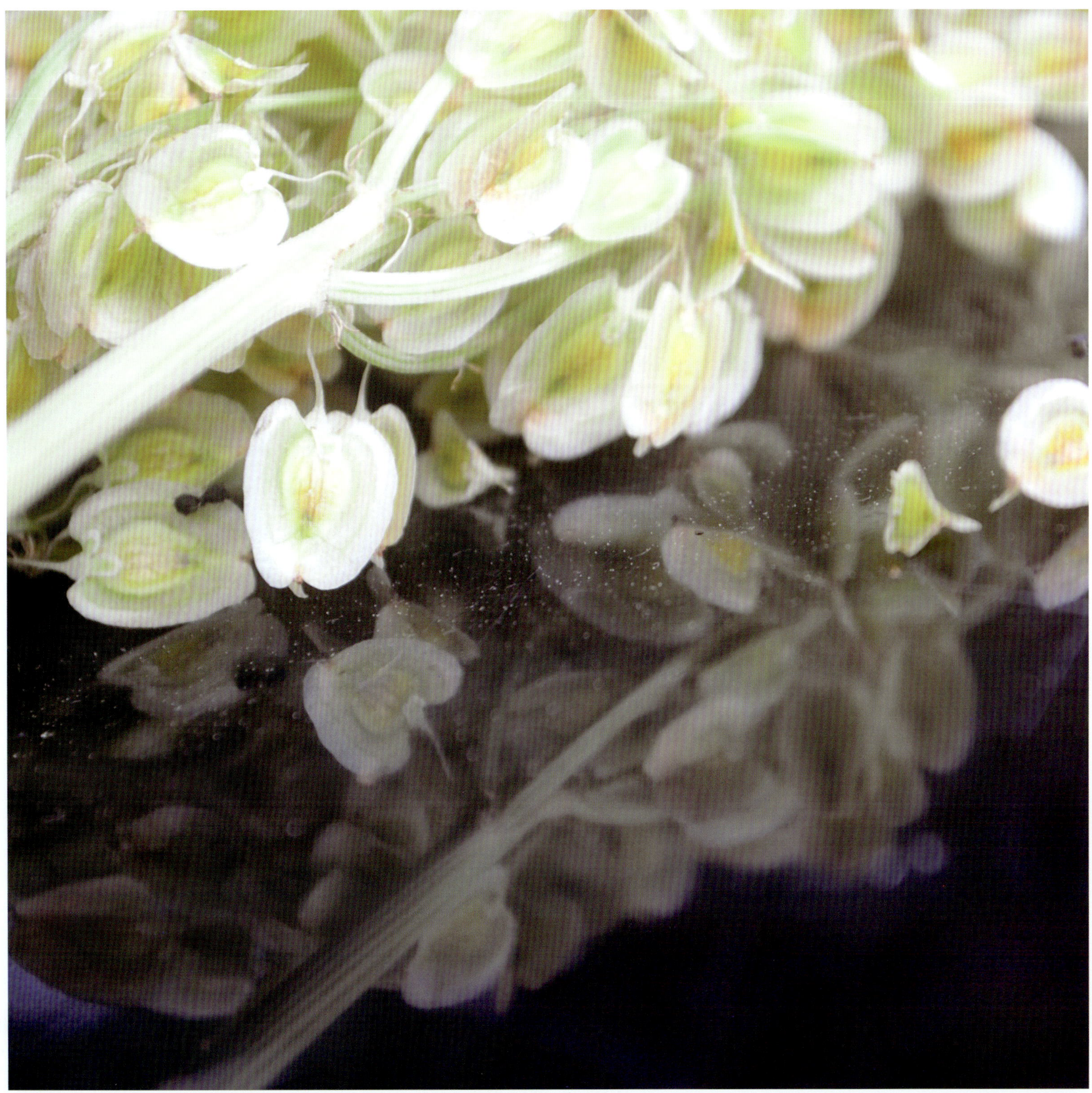

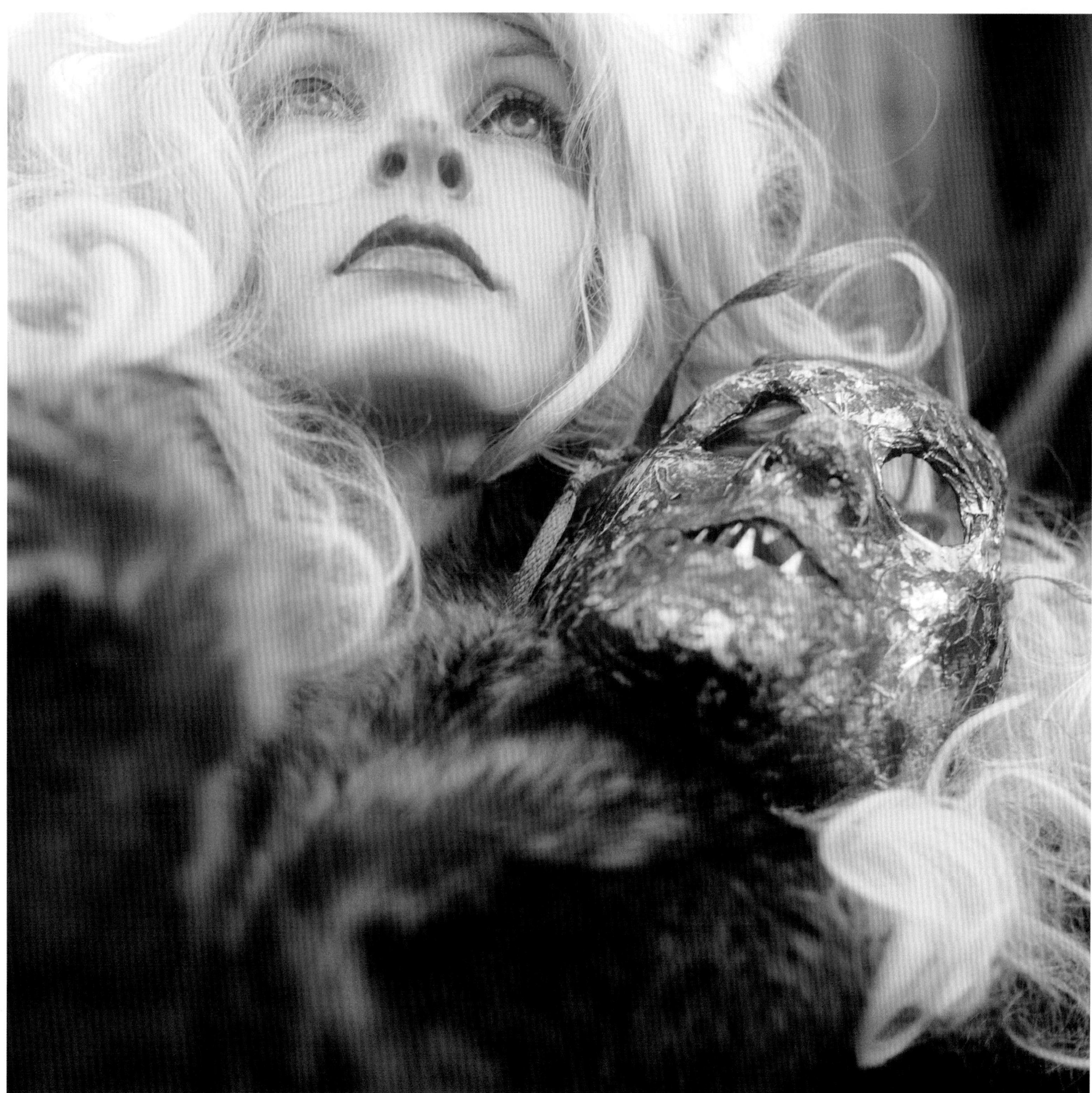

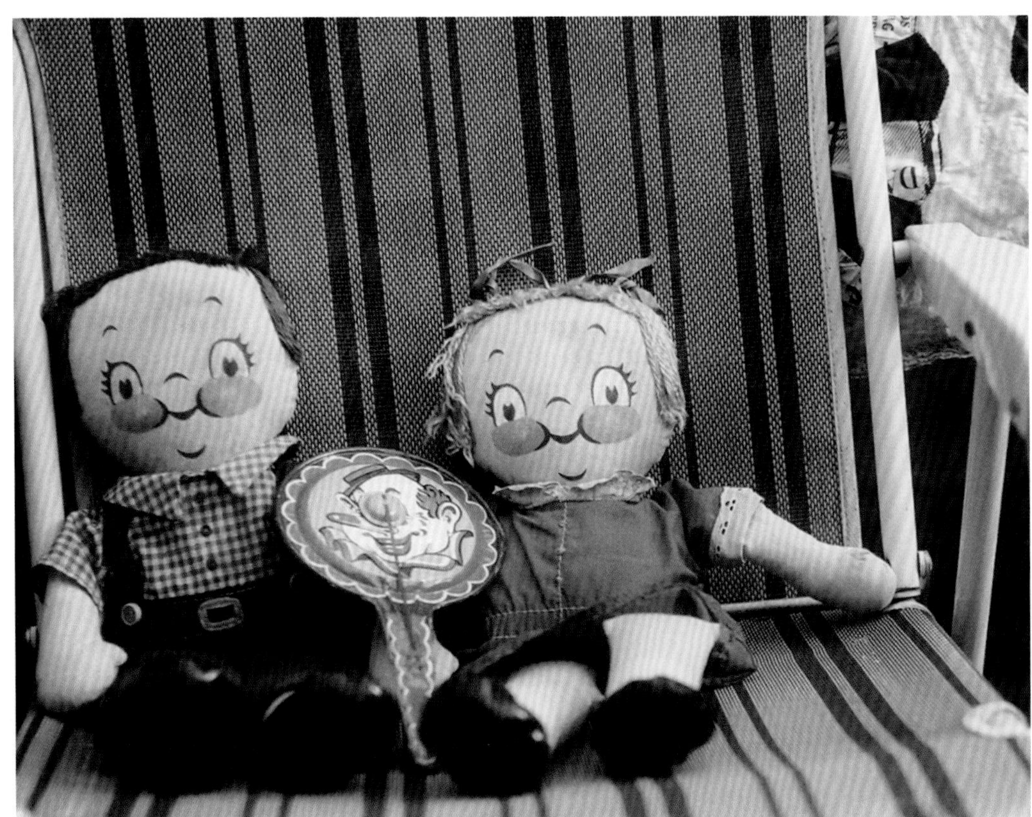

Contents

Photographs, Poems and Forget-Me-Nots from a Mainer Growing Up

Kristie Billings comes from a long line of lovers of the sea: fishermen, clamdiggers, and sardine packers. The ocean is home. She is a native of Stonington, Maine, currently living in Ellsworth.

Kristie is a poet, a photographer, and a year-round swimmer. A great lover of music, of art, and life, Kristie is drawn to beauty, even in the most ordinary, mundane way. She is drawn to what others may pass by, unnoticed.

Kristie has worn many hats over the years. She is a long time Saturday night DJ on Community Radio, WERU 89.9 FM, in Orland, Maine. From small town grocery clerk, to making tie dye t-shirts for the local import shop, to working at a fish market, or selling men's suits, owning her own shoe store. She was an Arts Educator at a local theater, and lobster fisher, barista, and antique seller.

Kristie is married to her best friend, Ed. They share a home with their rambunctious cats, who keep them on their toes.

Kristie is a collector. Of stories, of emotions, of dolls, of feelings, wigs, mannequin parts, record albums, memories, beauty, laughter, vintage clothing, scallop shells, barnacles, hermit crabs. She is an observer. She's been writing poetry since childhood, beginning with her love of Edna St.Vincent Millay to the Beat poets, Bukowski, and beyond. As for photography, she has been taking pictures for years, bought a used Nikon, and has proceeded to buy more cameras since then. She is drawn with awe to the artists that may make you uncomfortable.

Sea Witch, a photography and poetry book by Maine native, Kristie Billings – images and words of the sea, nature, folk art, dolls, loss, grief, love, acceptance, rage, music, life.

From punk rock to menopause to swimming with seals! A middle-aged story of *Sea Witch*.

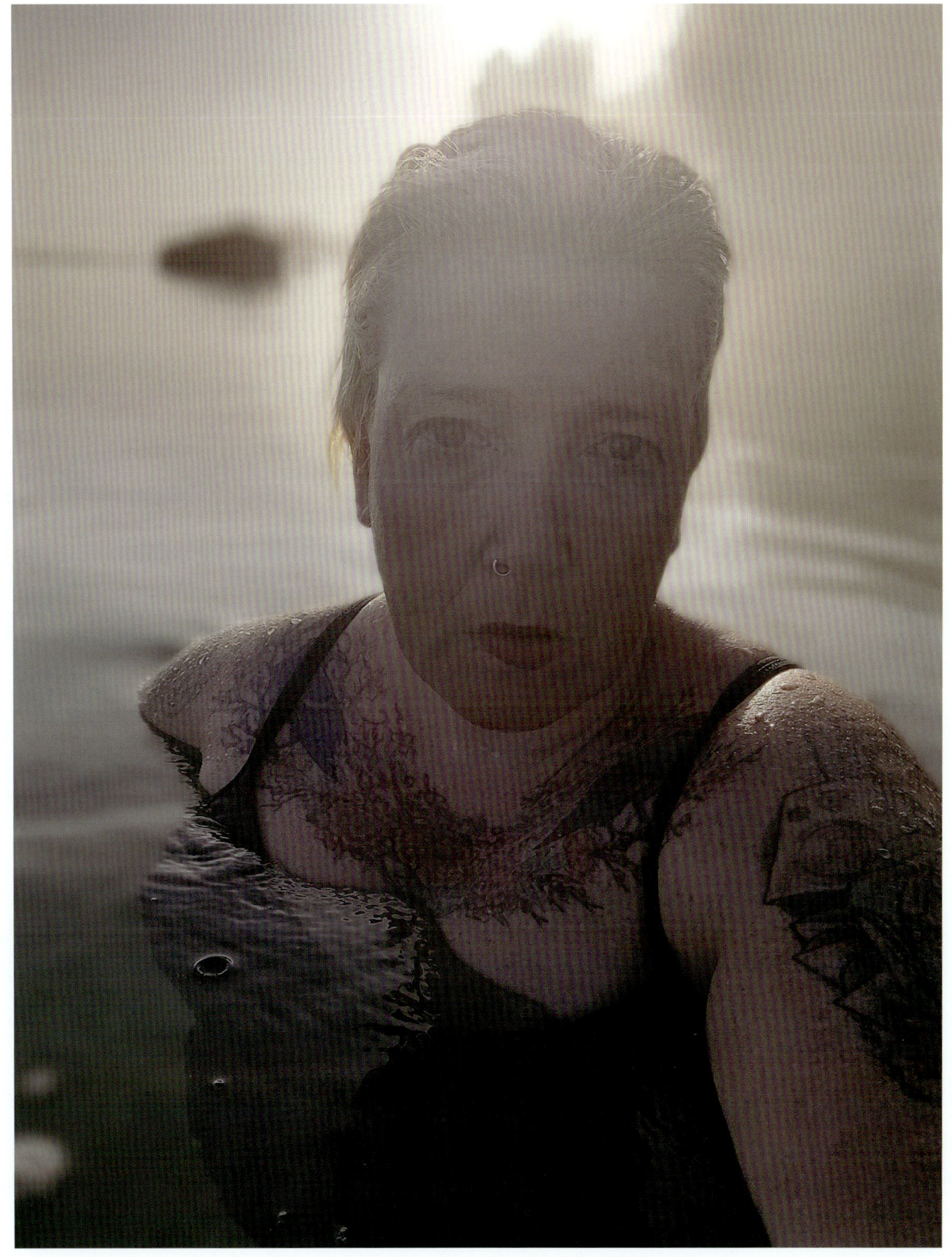

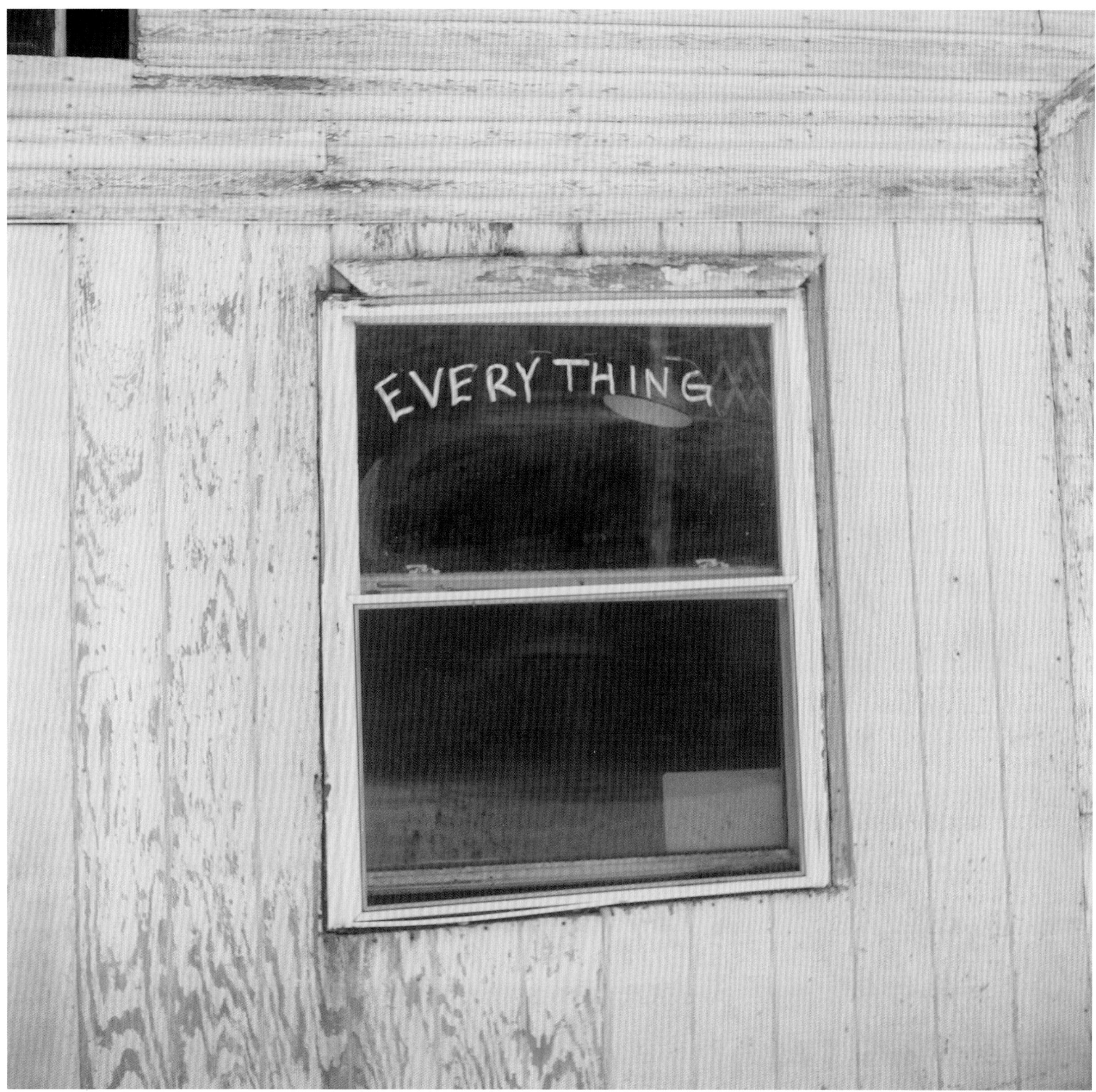
EVERYTHING

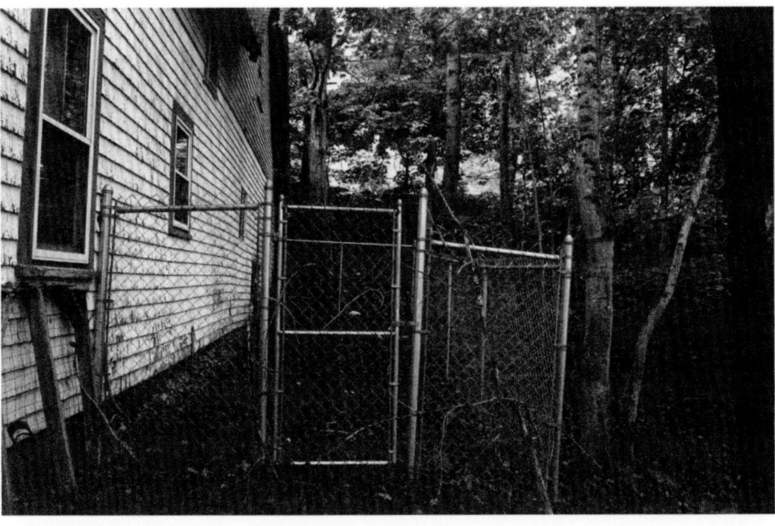

Welcome Home

While ocean swimming yesterday
A mild December day in Maine,
I giggled that it was good that I was an ample woman.
And this morning I feel like my breasts are
like yeast rolls.
My stomach is like boule.
I have risen.
I am salty and rich.
Wash me down with a big glass of water.
My lips and nipples are like a side of chutney.
My hair is dulse.
I offer my fruits to the sea.
I stand waist high in the water
And look toward the horizon.
No glasses on
But I can see
The gray truth.
The December light holding me.
The crows fly overhead crowing welcome back.
Seagulls drop their mussels on the ledges
And decide to swim near me
Watching me.
They know I'm not like the people who flood their
beaches in August shrilling.
We speak the same language.
The ocean is our home.
It's that simple.
I slip under the waves
Resurfacing with pink cheeks
And rock hard periwinkle nipples.
I giggle
Taking the ocean into my mouth and letting the salt roll
around my tongue,
My teeth,
My gums,
And squirt it back out with childlike glee.
Welcome home.

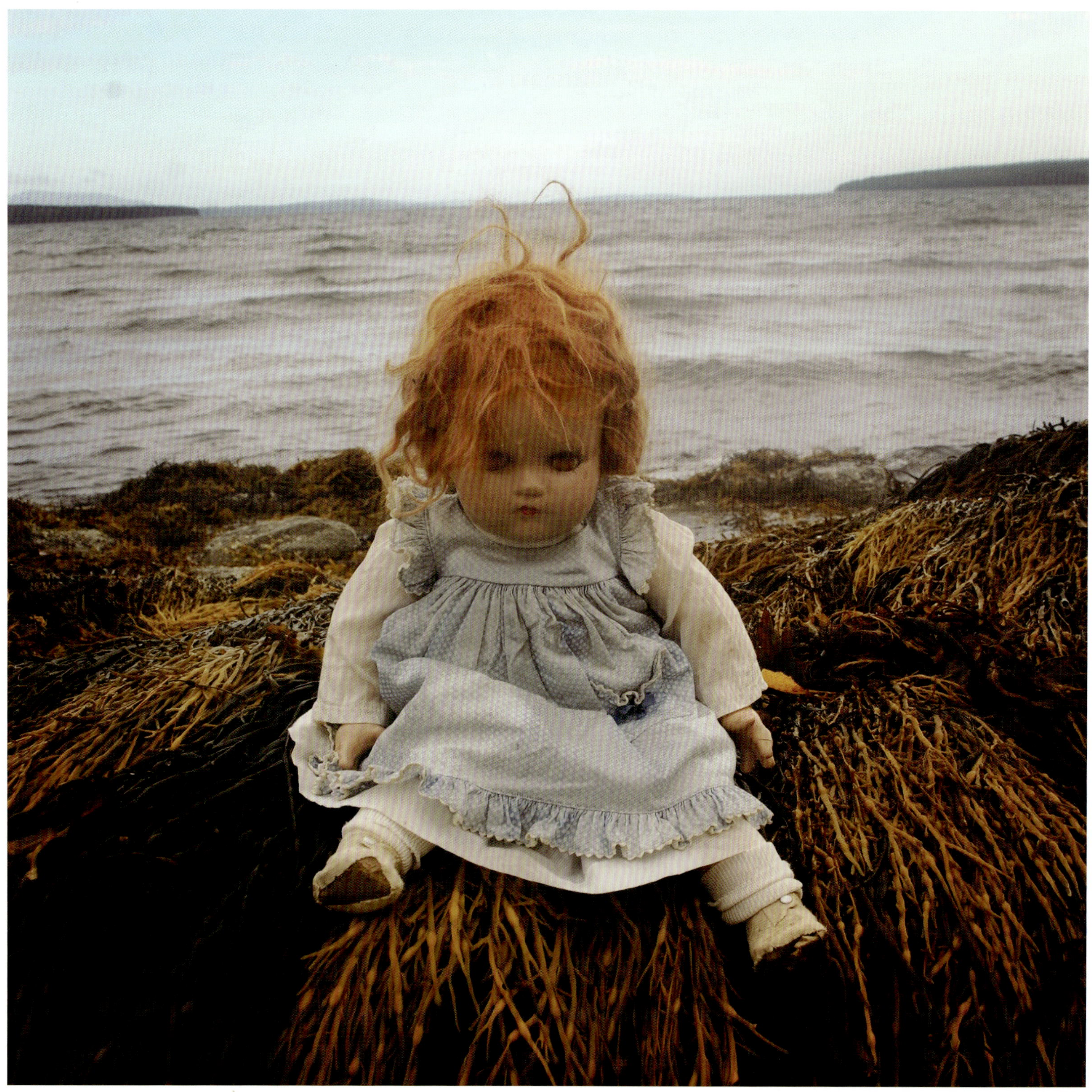

I slip under the waves
Resurfacing with pink cheeks
And rock hard periwinkle nipples.

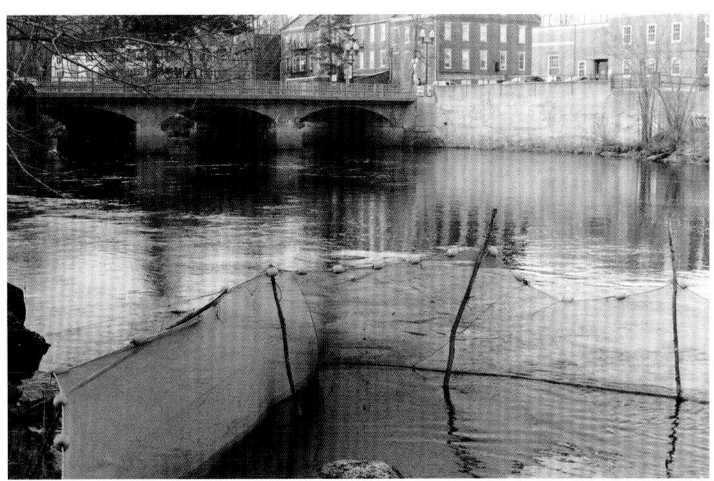

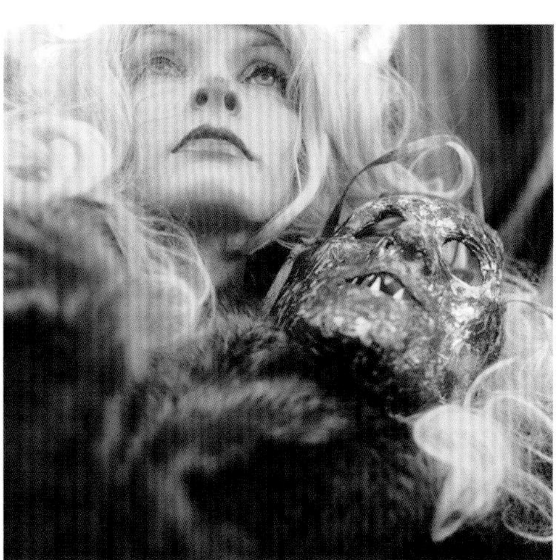

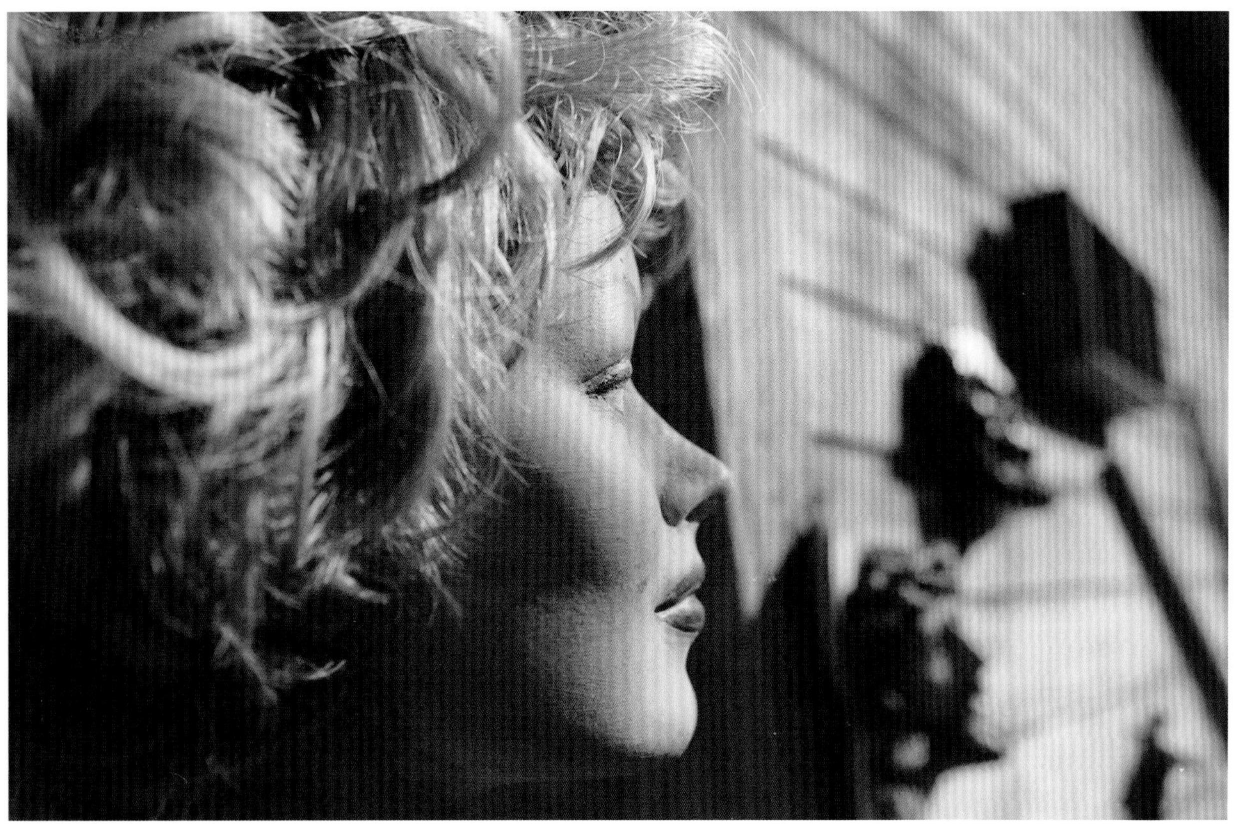

Sand Dollar

I'm the sand dollar you bleached
And have on your mantle
A reminder of something you hunted
And claimed as yours
But now sits dusty and idle
You should have left me in the ocean
Where I belong.
On the bottom
Covered in mud
But alive.

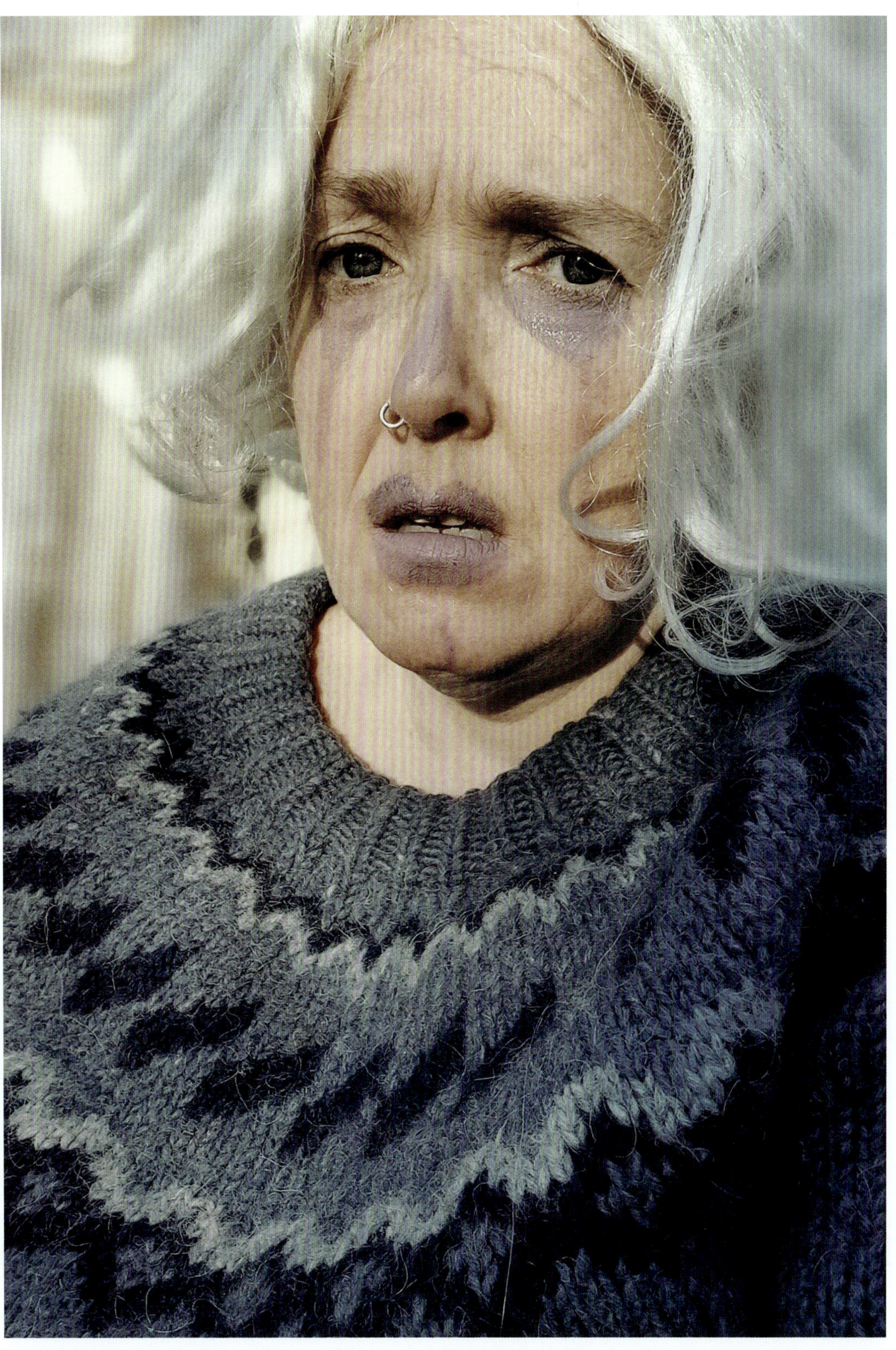

Poor So and So

Oh, poor poor so and so
Don't even have a pot to piss in
Oh, poor poor — family
They never had nothing
Except nothing
And heartache.
Oh, poor poor_____
She has had many misfortunes
She works so hard
Poor poor shit for brains
He ain't got a chance in hell!
I've been hearing this my whole life
You have too!
I can't figure out what's wrong with any of
these poor, poor people?
Do people say that about me?
Poor poor Kristie,
She ain't ever going anywhere.
Lord! That one's brain is jelly.
Stupid?
I'd say!
And she oh my word!
Have you seen her?
Her body
Is all jiggly
Wiggly
Like chopped up jello
In a big bowl of speckled confetti Texasware
in the backseat of your station wagon.
Daddy smoking one of his menthols
And the family dog is panting.
No AC
Your sister is pinching you
And your mama tells you to stop or your
daddy will let you out right here
Her body jiggles and wobbles.
And she isn't talented.
No way.
She just thinks she is.
She always thought that she was better than
us. Ha
She?
Oh yeah
Her!
Poor Poor so and so.
Her Mama and Daddy
Never been happy
Running around
Drinking
Never could save a dime
Yeah, she lives in a trailer
Works real hard
Really hard
She'll never get ahead
Poor Poor
Poor.
And that one!
God did that girl drink!
And she drank
Did all the drugs
Let men use her
Abuse her
Beat her.
And now she has a disabled kid
I heard she drank
Did drugs
Throughout her pregnancy!
Her kid isn't right, they say.
That's what you get for that kind of
behavior.
I heard she's back in school
Oh yeah?
I doubt she'll make it.
That poor kid
Having her as her Mama
Yeah, it doesn't stand a chance
Heard the baby daddy has 6 other kids
With other women
Heard he has a bad bad temper
Well, he's fishing
At least
Yeah, he had a rough upbringing
His daddy was so and so
A hardworking fisherman.
Poor poor
Poor
Vaping
Drinking
Smacking your kid
Scanning your mac and cheese Looking at
your big screen TV Scrolling
Trolling
Gossiping
Poor poor
Me.
Lord!
Poor me.
Sitting here
Judging.

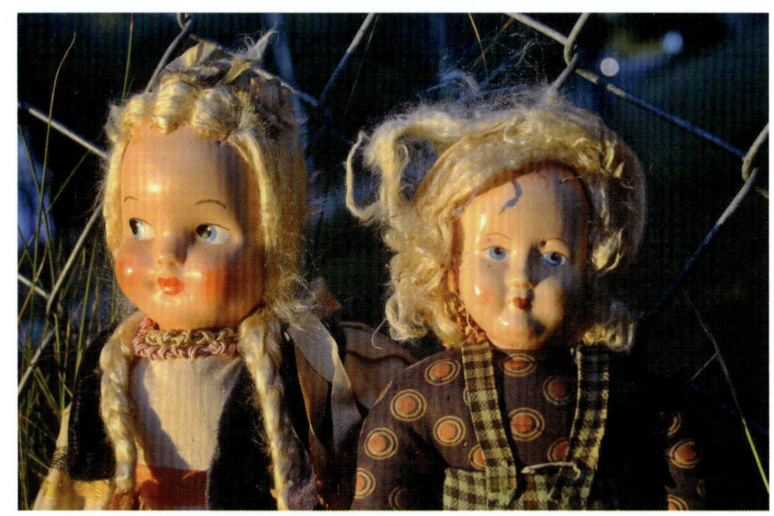

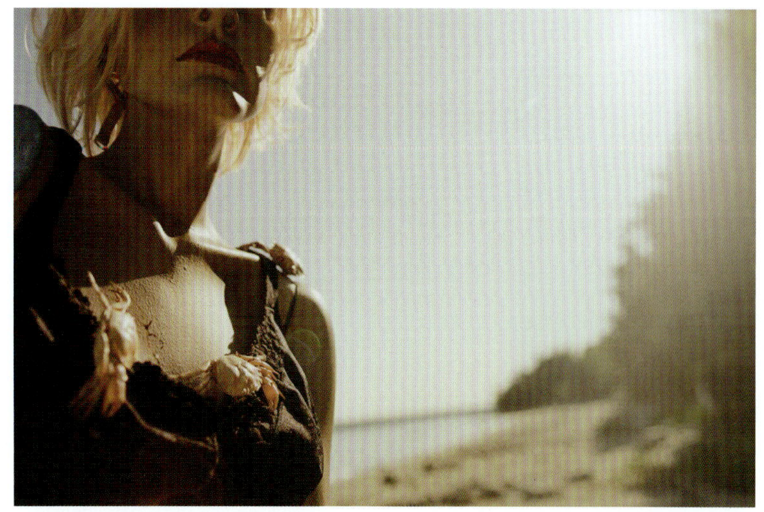

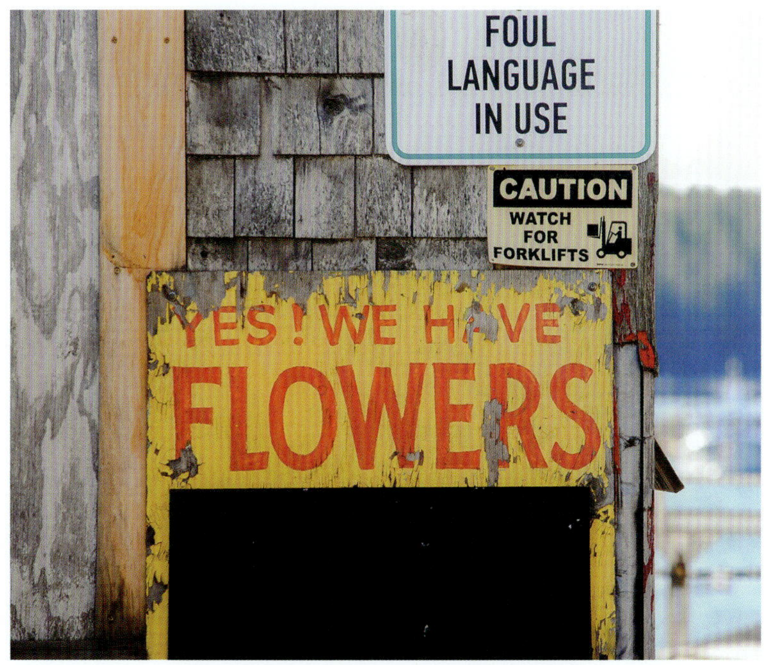
FOUL
LANGUAGE
IN USE
CAUTION
WATCH
FOR
FORKLIFTS
YES! WE HAVE
FLOWERS

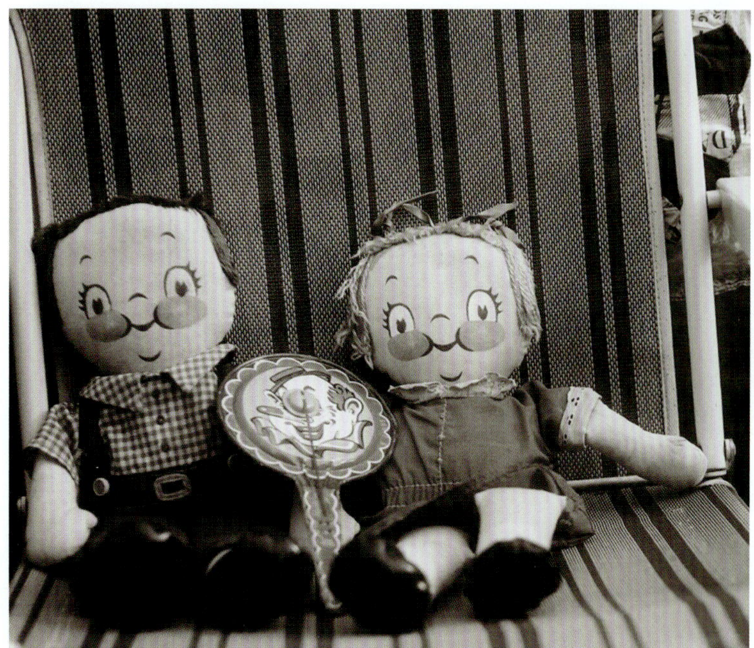

Lord!
Poor me.
Sitting here
Judging.

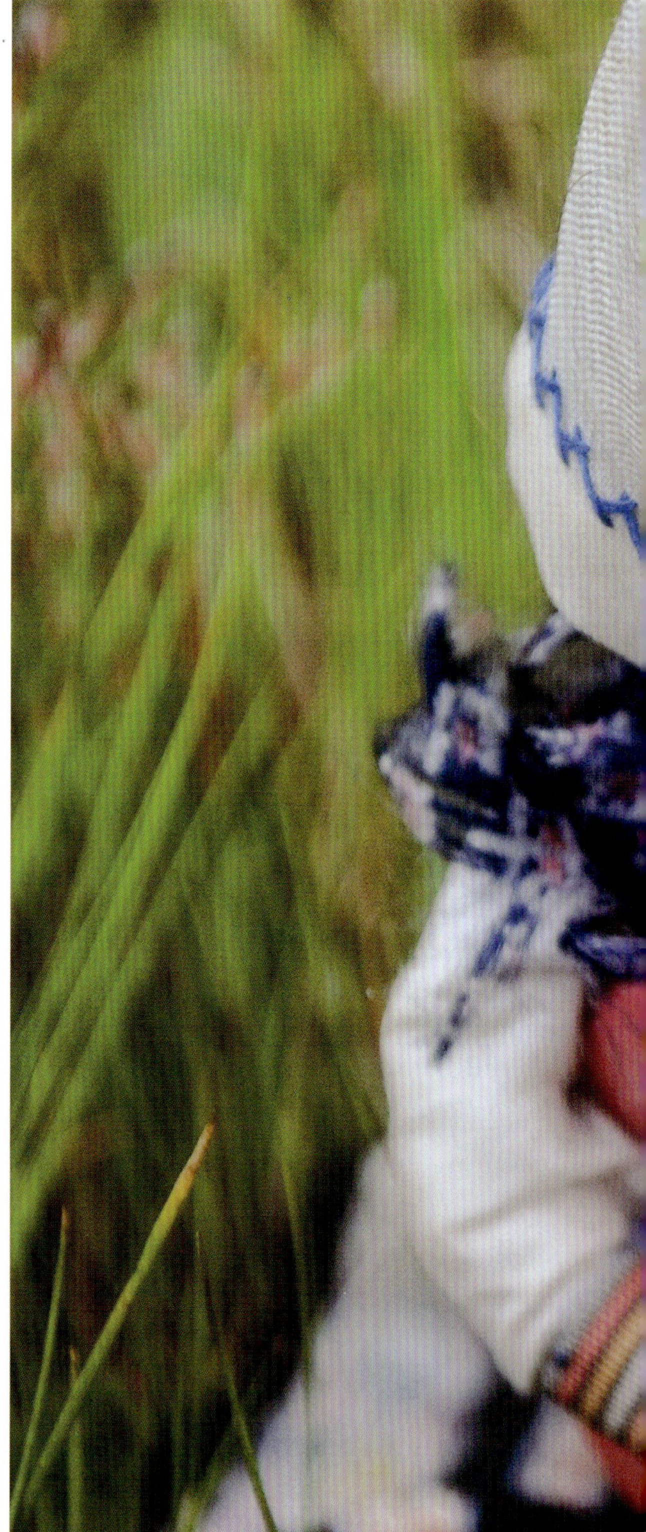

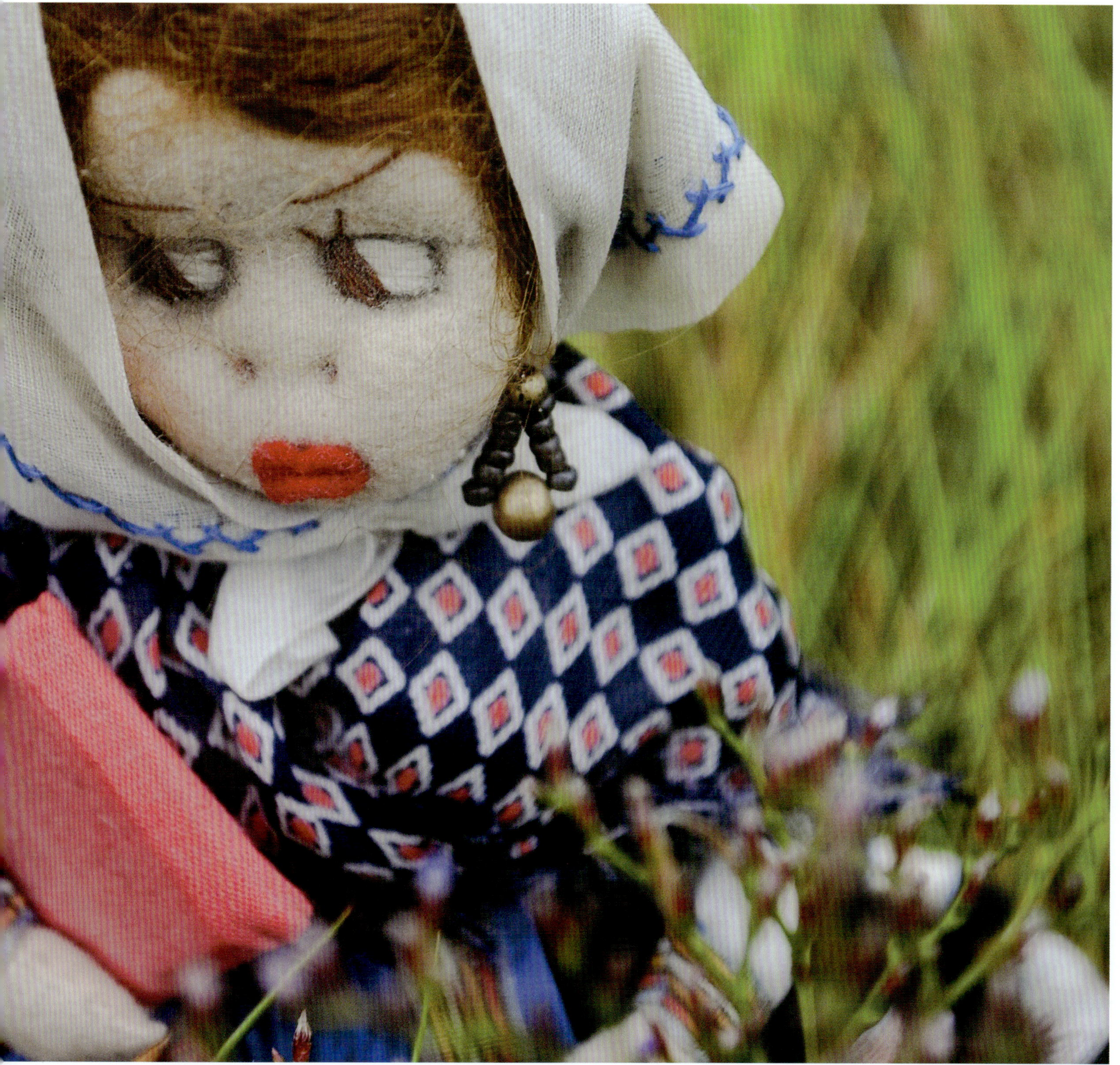

My Big Thighs

My big thighs.
I once vowed
Never to get fat again.
My big belly
Big round face
Everything BIG
Like my goober heart.
All my damn problems
After my Dad died.
I tried to protect my Mom
Protect her from what?
I guess getting hurt
Again
How idiotic
How foolish
Like me saying I'd never get fat
again.
Because I'm not young.
Menopause and me are TIGHT
Like seam splitting!
Like muscles aching!
Anxiety and Insomnia RICH!
Protect her!
Don't get fat again!
No more hurt!
Now everything has gone to
shit.
It's always
Shit
With beautiful flickers
Sunsets that make you oooh.
Babies that make you ahhhhh
Music art nature
And cheese,
And
chips
Beer too
make your mouth water.
It isn't fun getting older
I've heard this my entire life!
But I know it to be FACT.
Now I understand not wanting
to go out
How I can't handle drinking too
much
That I love my bathrobe
That certain foods do make me
feel bad
And how I can say NO to things
Thank the LORD
Or whatever.
I said to someone
Anyone
Somebody
Myself
Who knows
I never had children
I never really wanted to be a
Mama.
Except to my pets.
I'm totally cool with this.
I now feel like a parent
I'm super uncomfortable in this
role
Like really really fucking un-
comfortable.
But here we are.
I'm fat.
I didn't protect anyone
From getting hurt
And I'm a parent
More or less
And hot flashes aren't fun
Estranged family aren't great
In fact they suck.
But there are flickers
Flashes
I'll take them
And I'll cry a lot
Swear a lot
Fart
Laugh
Dance my fat ass around
Because what else is there
Really?
What else.

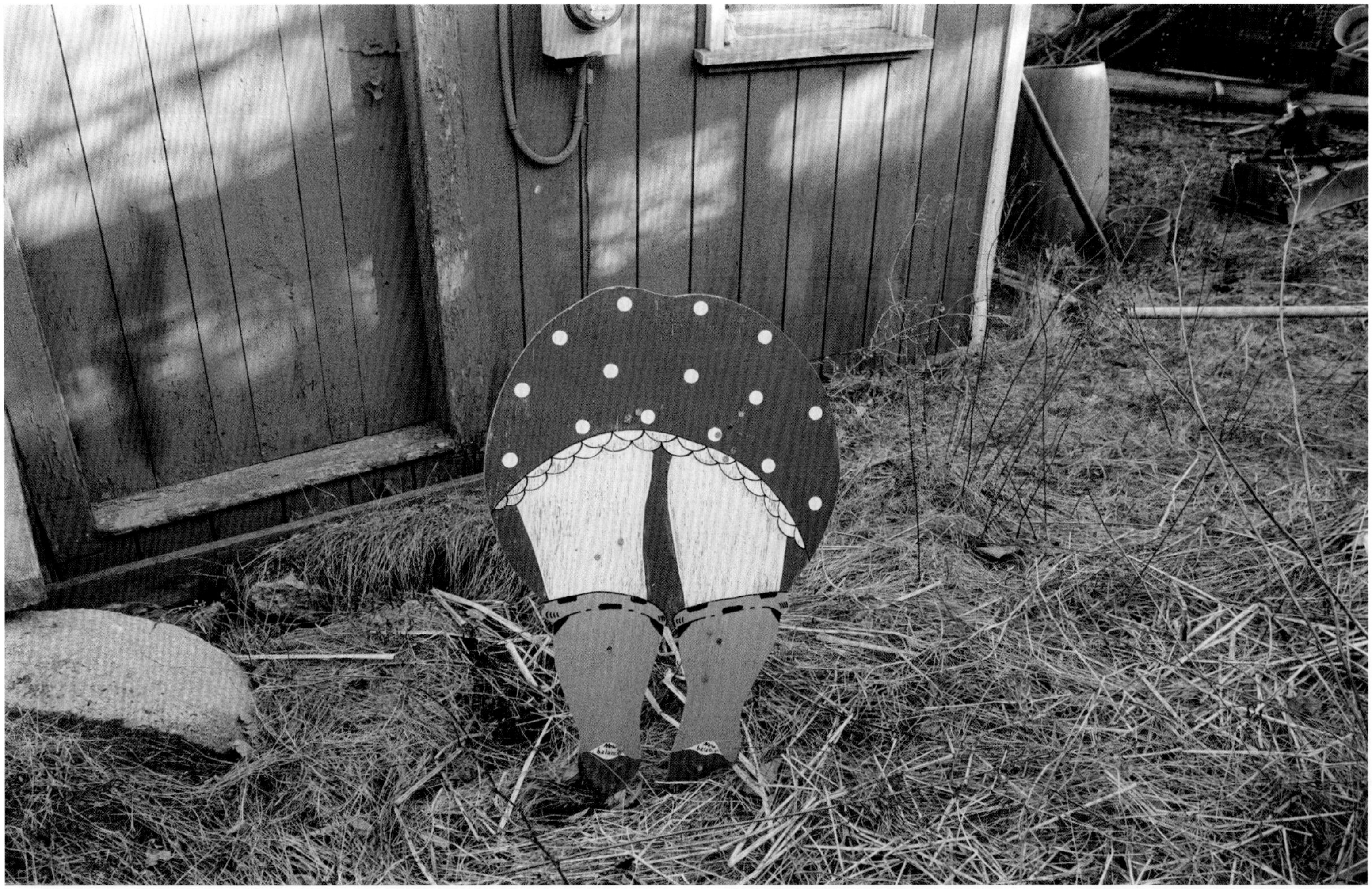

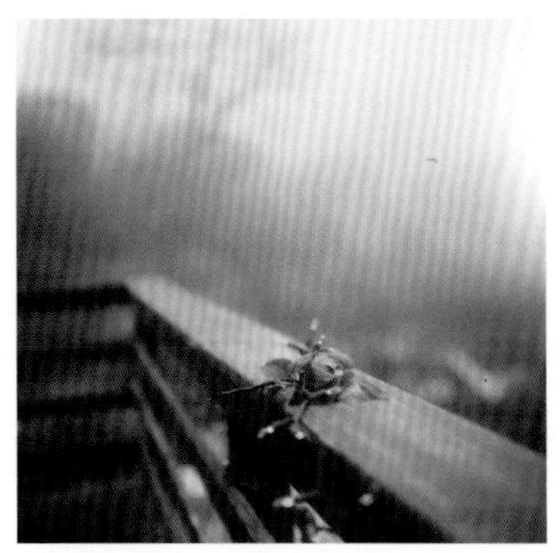

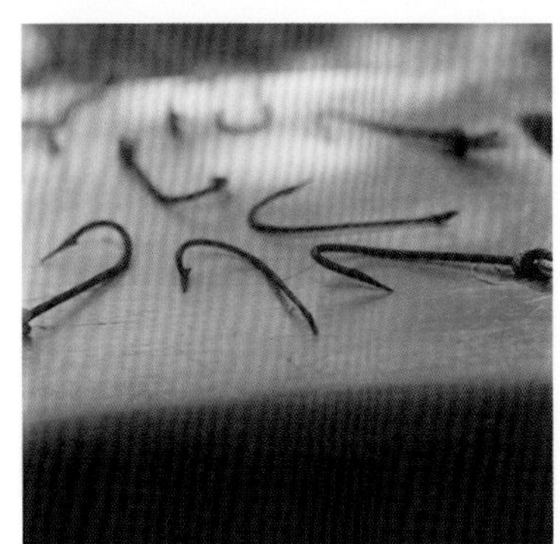

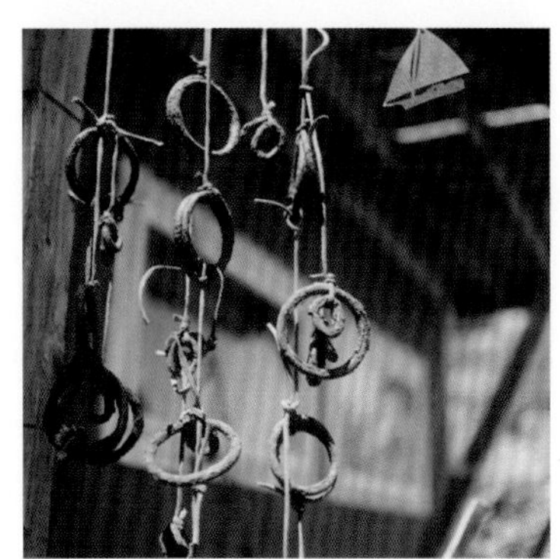

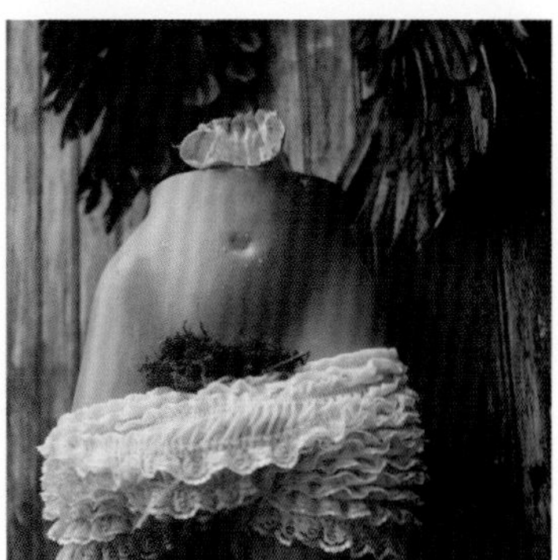

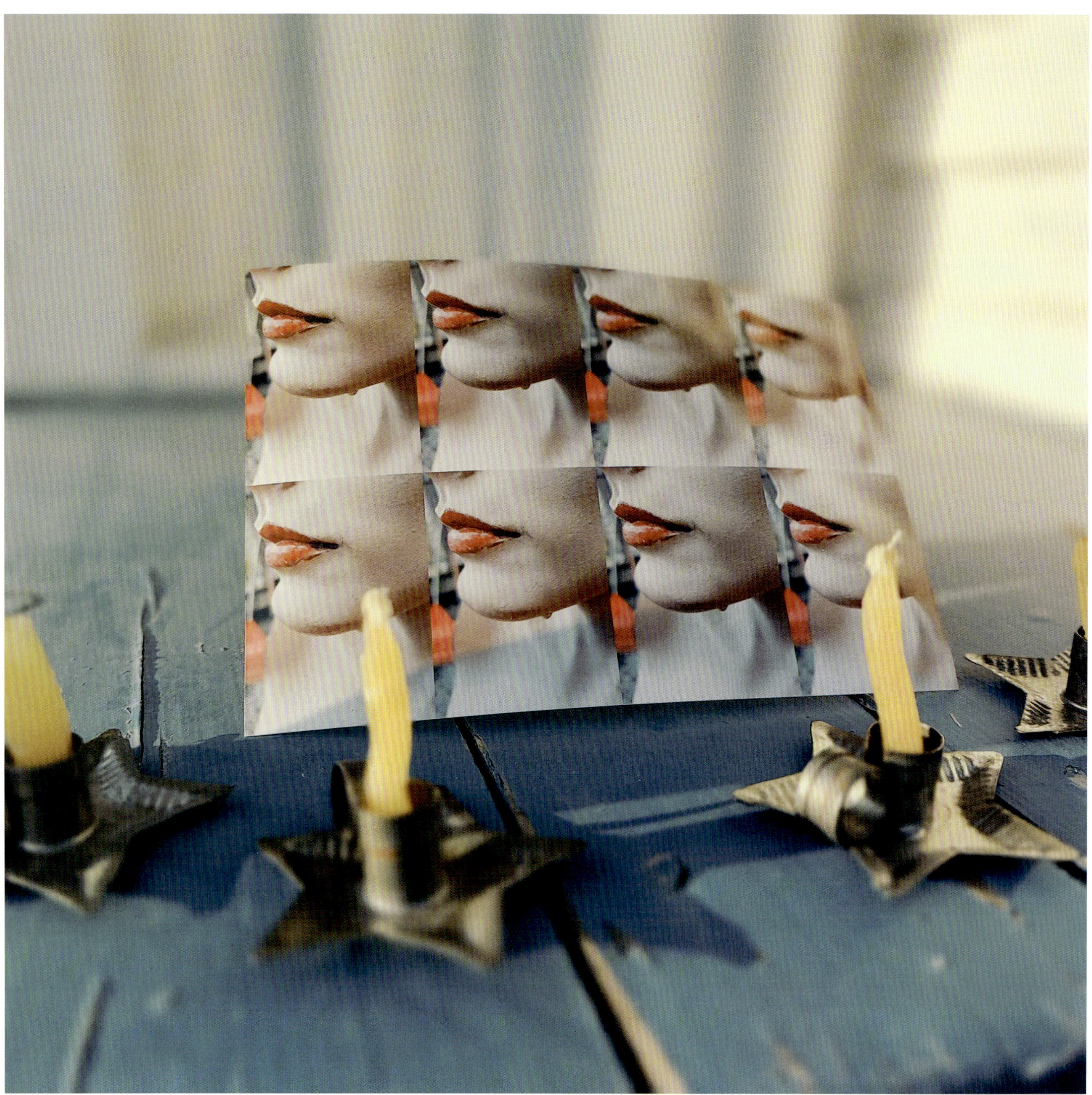

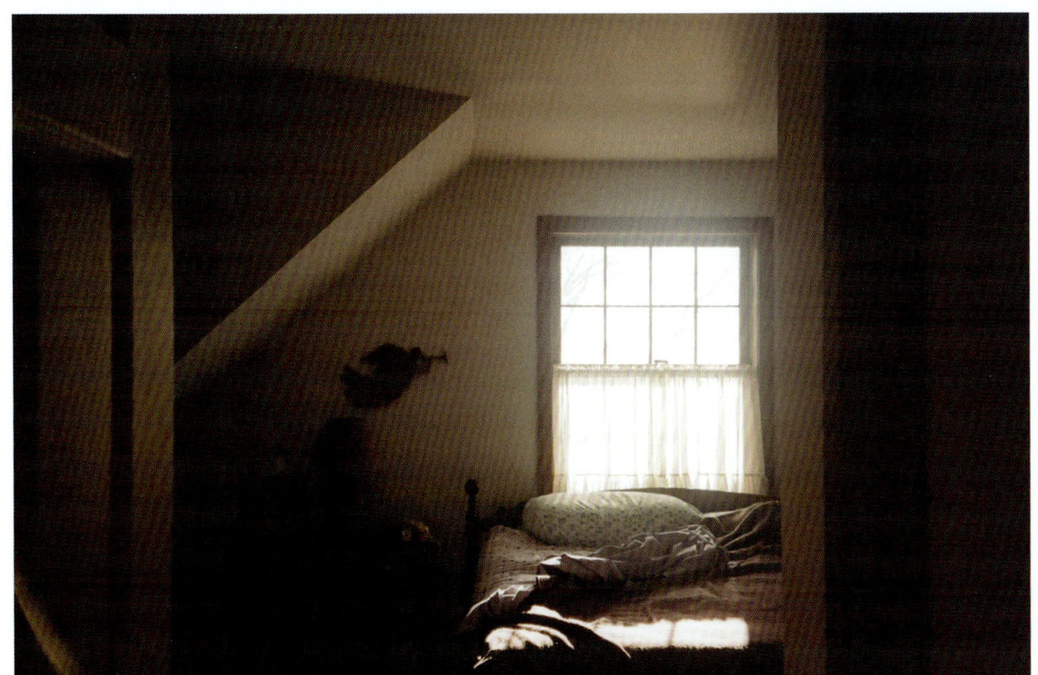

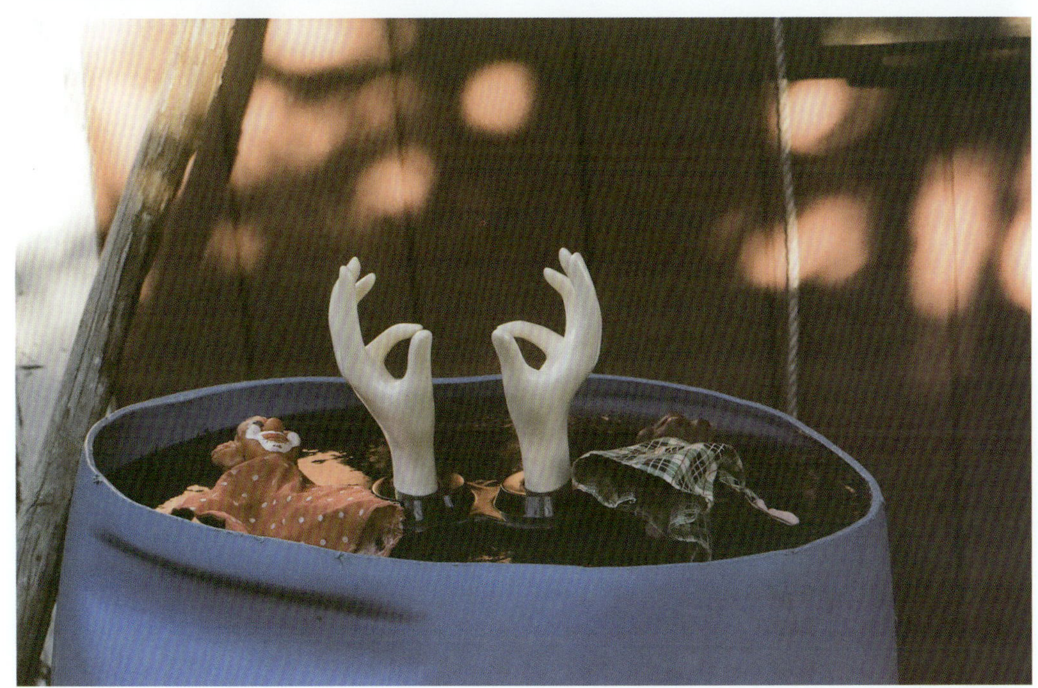

Everybody Loves You

“Kristie, Everybody loves you,
For you.
Don’t you know that?
Except maybe your sister.
Sorry, I had to.”

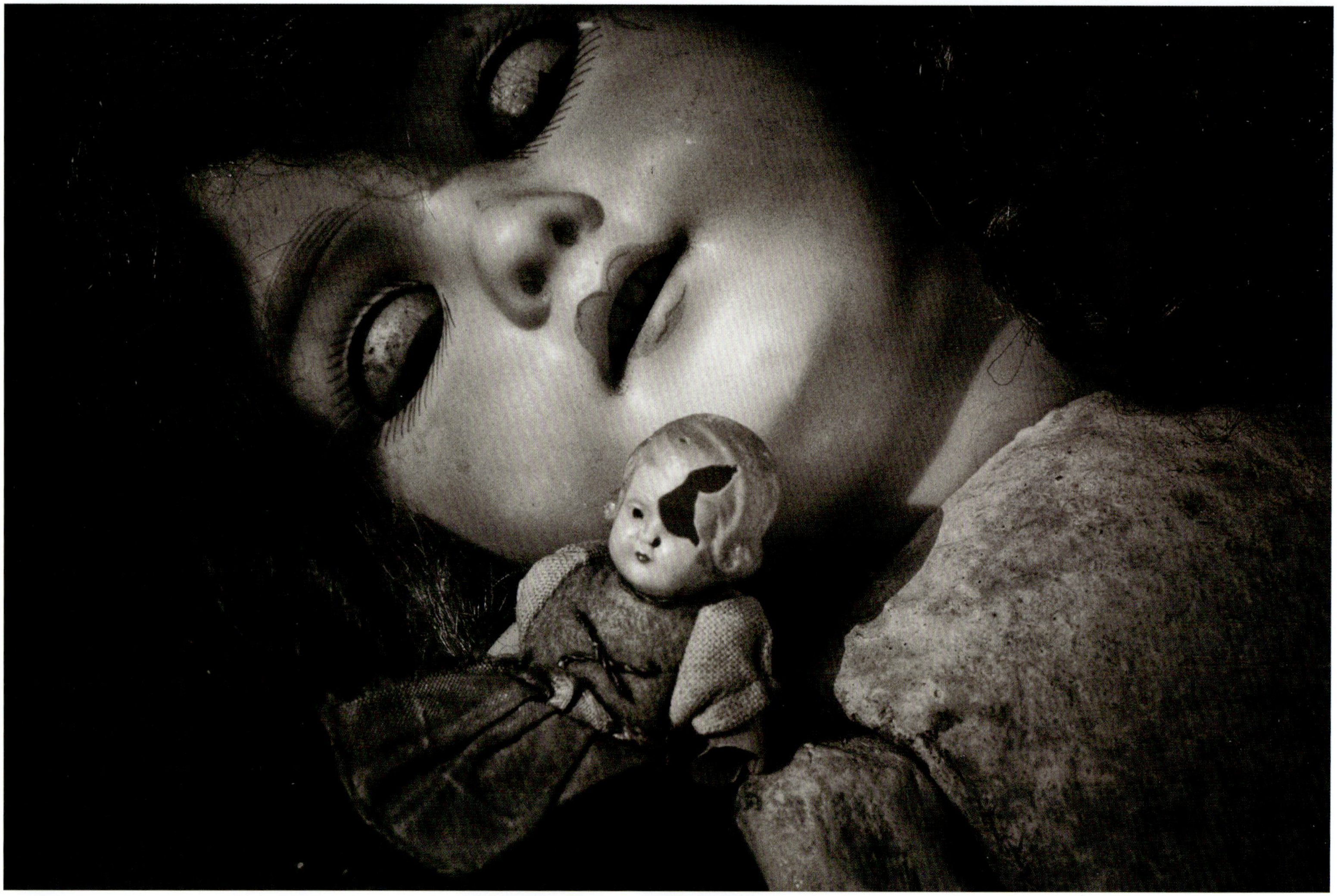

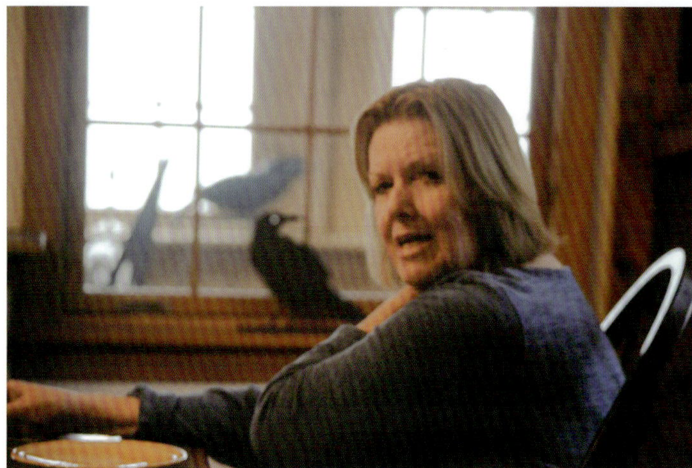

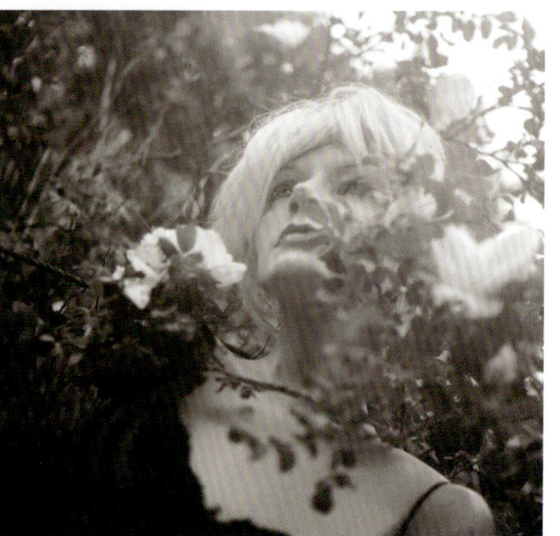

Caregiver

Like the blind leading the blind
Navigating
Through the dark storms
And this is just a mile down the road.

I have holes in my shirt
My skirt
I have a rash all over my body
I scratch
I itch
Feeling like I'm covered
In bugs
With spiders
Ticks
Nothing there.

Everyday I have a to do list
No completions
Just more added to it.

Caregiver.
We are only in about to our knees
Tripping over rocks
In churned up seas
Cutting up feet
Trying to maneuver
Without falling.
I never gave birth
To a baby
I gave birth
To love
To life
To worry
To being there.
Sometimes my two hands don't feel like
enough
Or strong enough
But they will do.
They hold you tenderly.
Navigating through dark storms.
We walk carefully around barnacle covered
rocks in churned up seas.
I hold your hand
And look at you softly smiling.
I'm here.

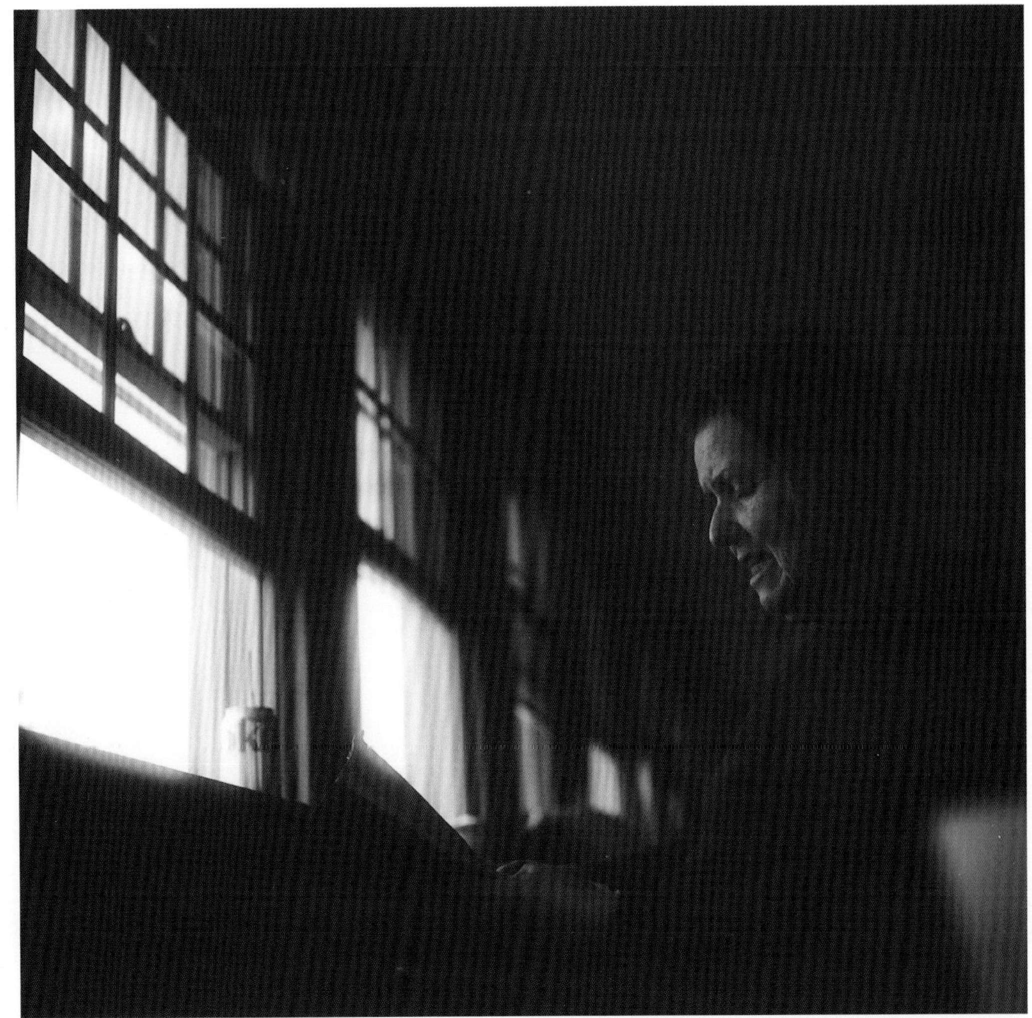

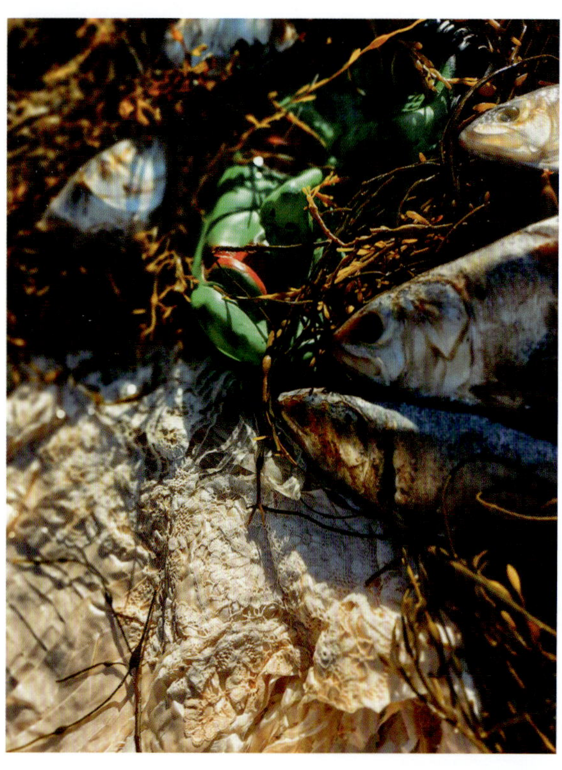

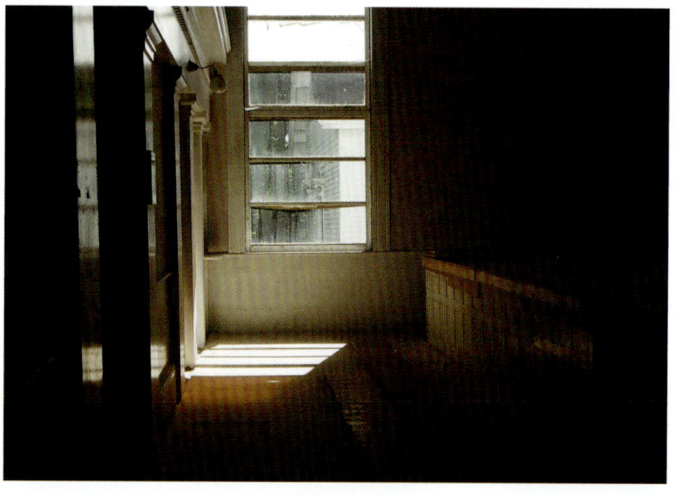

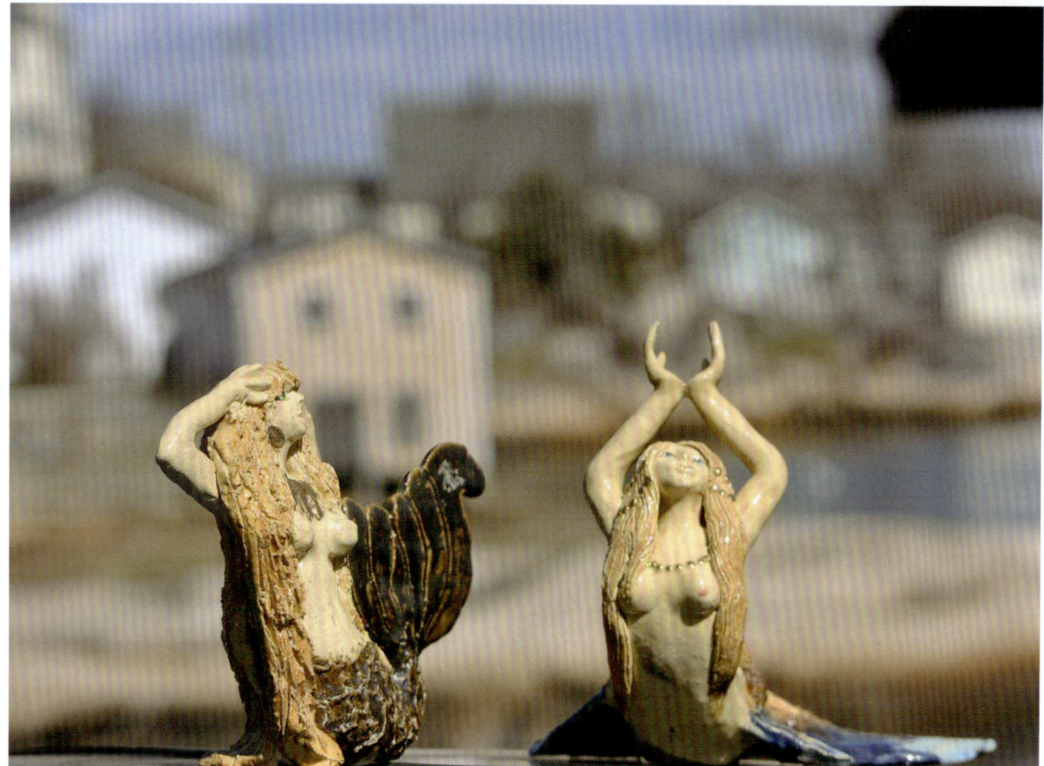

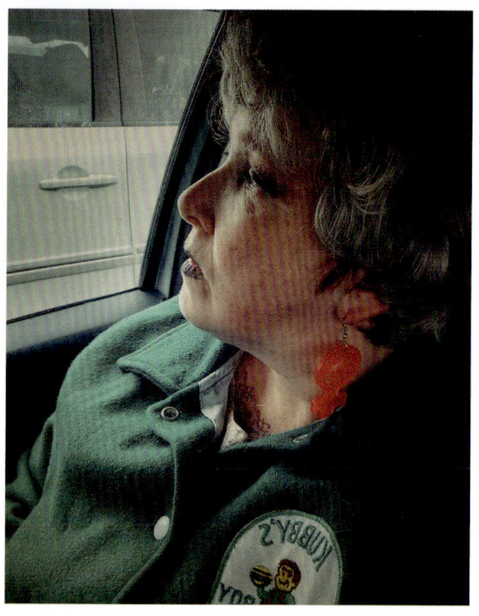
KUBBY'S

Meet Me

Meet me:
I'm a middle-aged white woman
From Maine,
A history of depression and anxiety,
Funny, sarcastic, loving, an empath.
Loves: nature, animals, poetry, art, music.
Dislikes people.
The things I think of with needles sticking in flesh:
I think of me as a teenager,
My childhood bedroom.
I think of how I get tired of seeing posts of kids on social media,
Babies spitting up all over themselves.
It makes me cringe,
How folks are traveling,
Spending gobs of money on all sorts of things,
People getting ready for Christmas.
I see me as a young woman.
And now lying here getting acupuncture
Because of bad knees
And perimenopausal symptoms.
I see myself in a hospital gown
With three other women,
All older,
All wearing purple gowns that tie in the front.
Mammograms
We share this experience
Yet we all sit there silent
Like we are praying in Church,
Hands folded in laps,
Looking at the floor,
The wall art,
Or mental pictures of things that we have to do.
I think of my love of men
How I have had a type ever since I can remember.
How their jaws have opened and called my name.
Over the phone,
In the dark,
In bars,
Kristie.
How their jaws have taken my heart
And shredded it to bits.
Like great white sharks.
My heart is like seaweed now with seafoam.
My husband is a blue whale.
As for me?
I'm not sure.
I think back to years ago as a girl.
A family picnic on an island.
A cookout on the beach.
Our family dog, Troubles, chased an island sheep into the water.
The sheep drowned.
I remember my Dad trying to save it.
I was crying.
Begging, "Please save the sheep, please."
Time to strip the bed
Time for laundry.
To wash up.
To put on clean clothes.
And be thankful.
I can hear the whales singing,
The trees moaning,
The cats purr.
Now turn your head this way
Push your breast up, out, for imaging.
The clinician says you're doing fine.
You smile behind your cloth mask.
Thankful for her kindness,
We all sit alone, hands folded in laps,
Exposed,
Waiting for our name to be called.

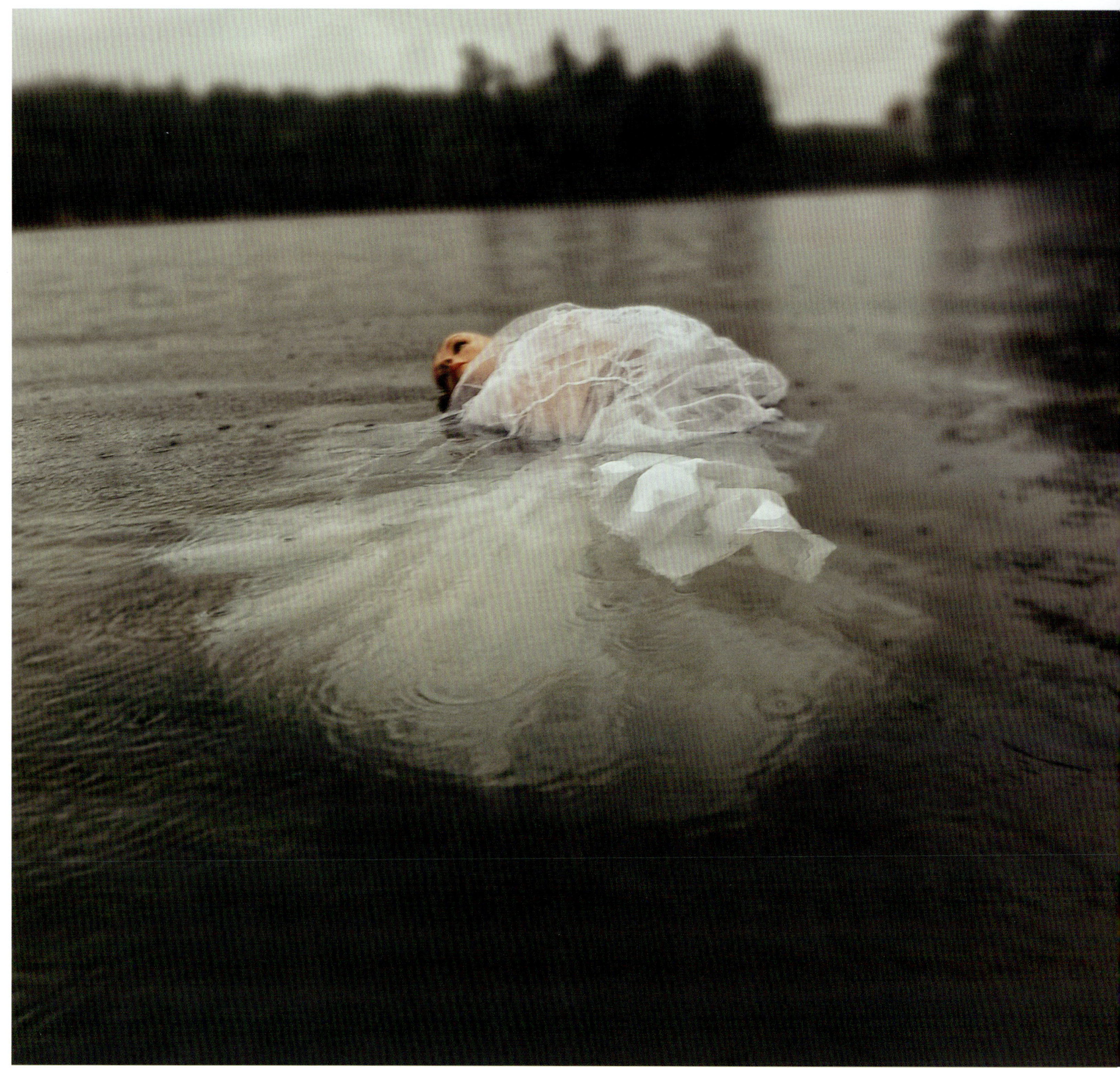

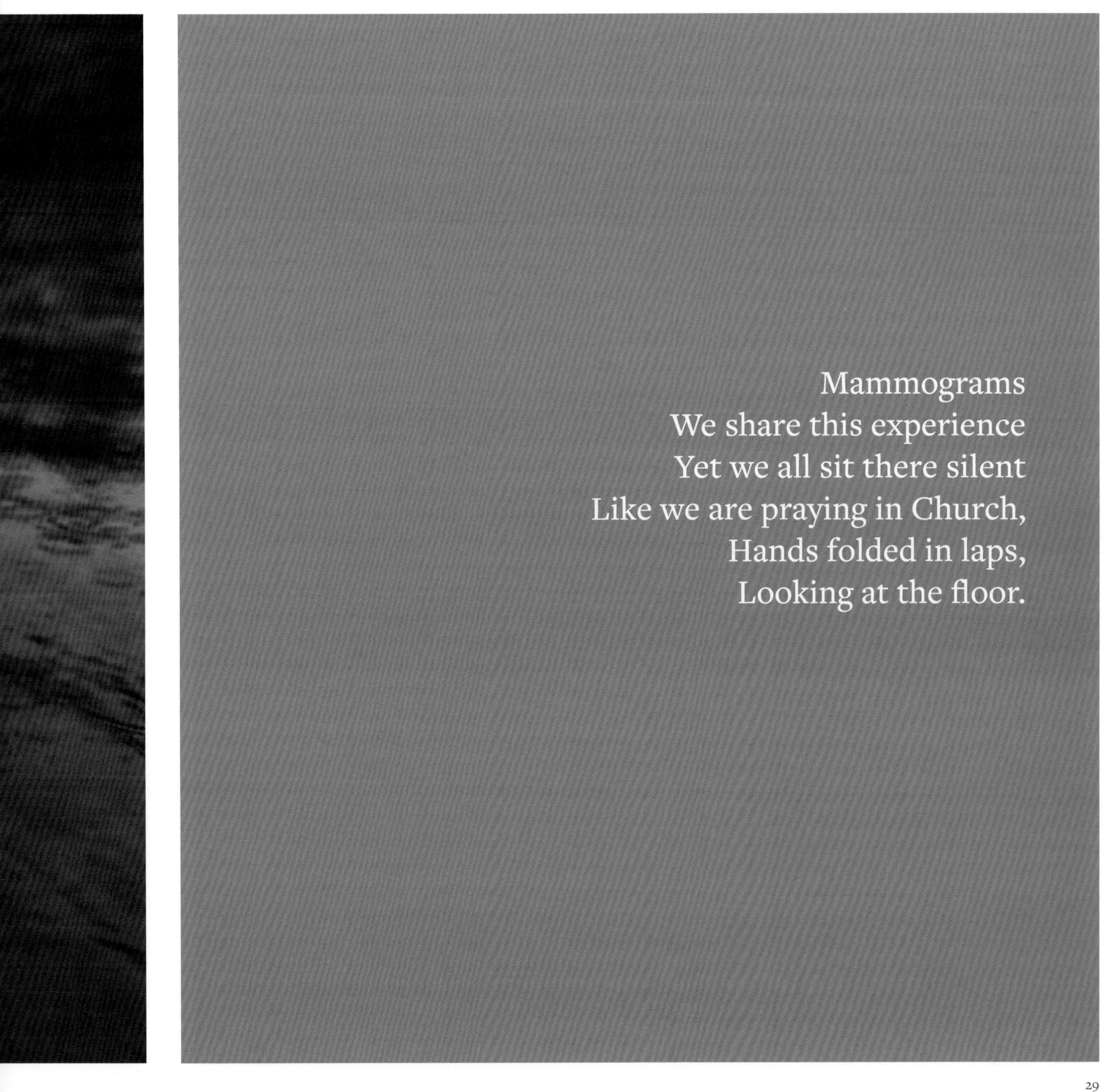

Mammograms
We share this experience
Yet we all sit there silent
Like we are praying in Church,
Hands folded in laps,
Looking at the floor.

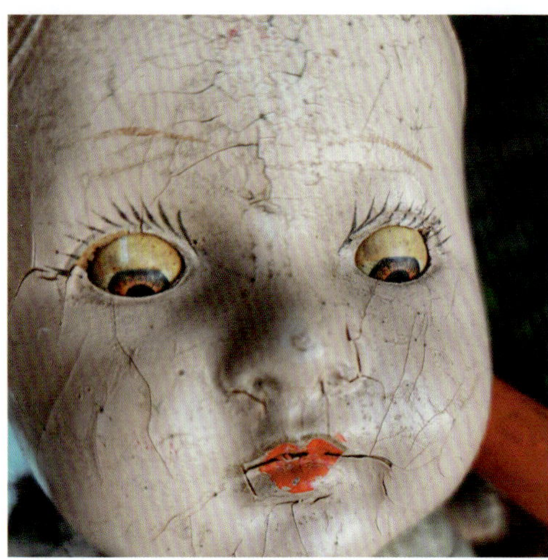

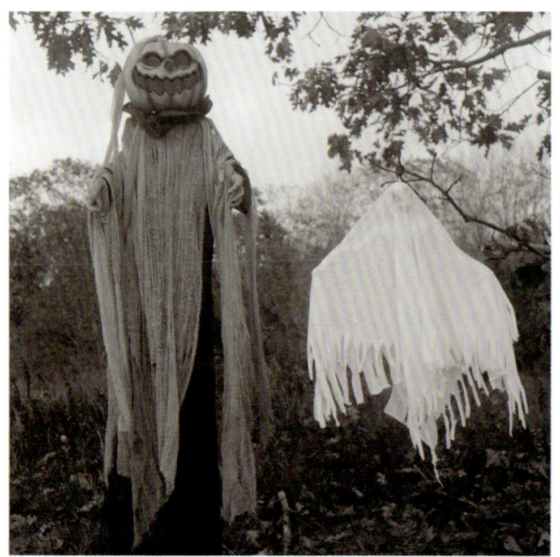

Salvage Diver

I imagine what it would be like
To be a salvage diver.
Under the water.
The vast
Darkness.
Wreckage.

To find my earrings
My barrettes
And bandaids
In the shallows

What would I find
Among the bottles
Chains
And rope.

Would I find myself?
My childhood.
Tire swings
Rusted gymsets
Bicycles
Corduroy Overalls
Butterfly wings
And popsicle sticks.
Tiny diary keys
Plastic lunchboxes
Jump rope
Matchbox cars
Training wheels
And bibles.

Would I find old record albums
Broken TVS
Rotary phones
Disco balls
My first car.
Would I find the remains of drowned
fishermen
from my town?
Lobster gear?
Scallop drags?
Boats,
Airplanes?

Would I find my answers
Would I finally blink back
All the darkness
All the sadness
And get some goddamn rest?

Nobody knows
Nothing
A goddamn thing
You just gotta play it by ear
Wing it.
20 years ago
I had a gun pointed at me.
I made it.
I'll make this too.
Someday I won't.
That's okay.
You'll find me wrapped in seaweed.
With a seal close by
Knowing
Something
That was my heart.

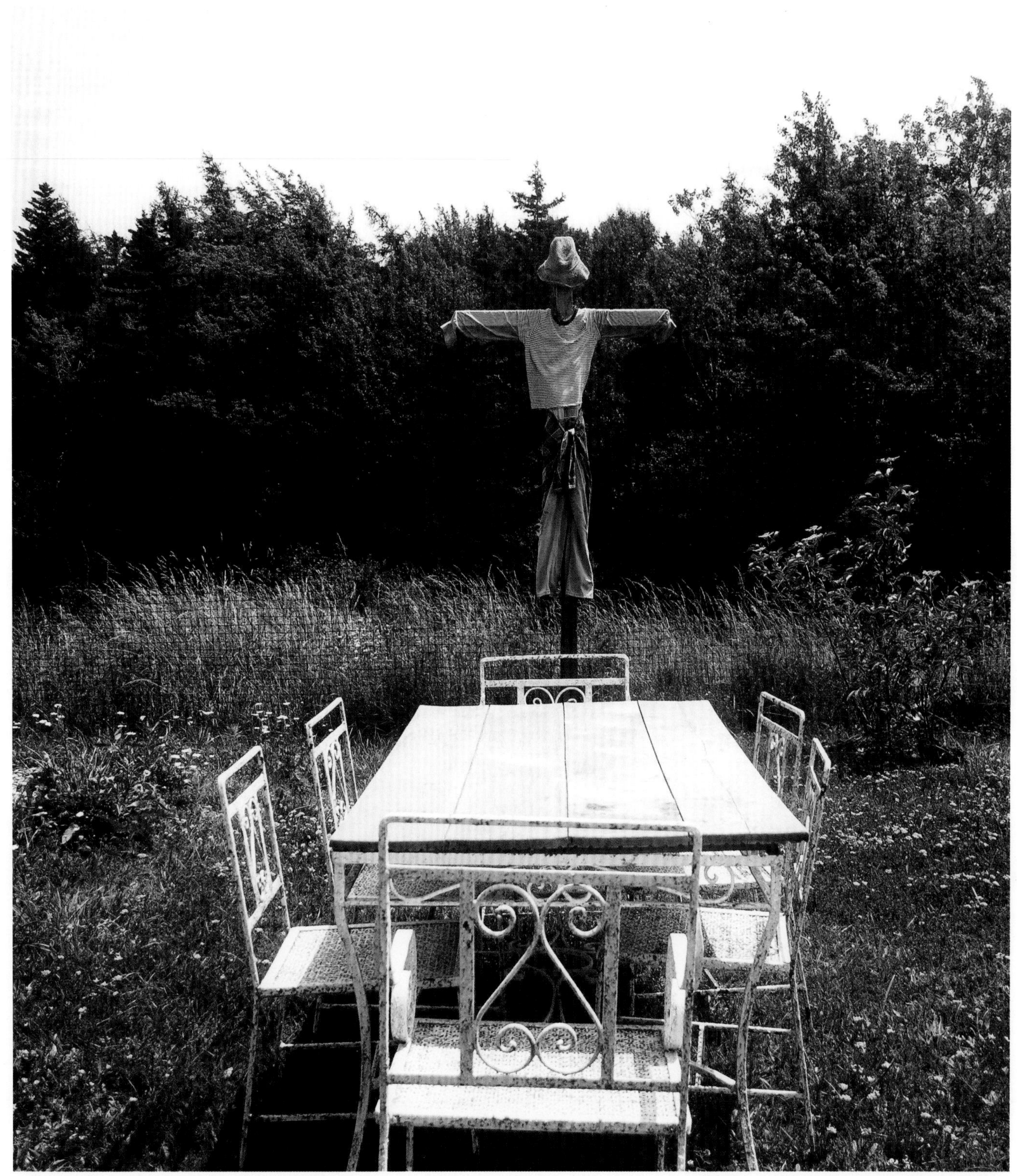

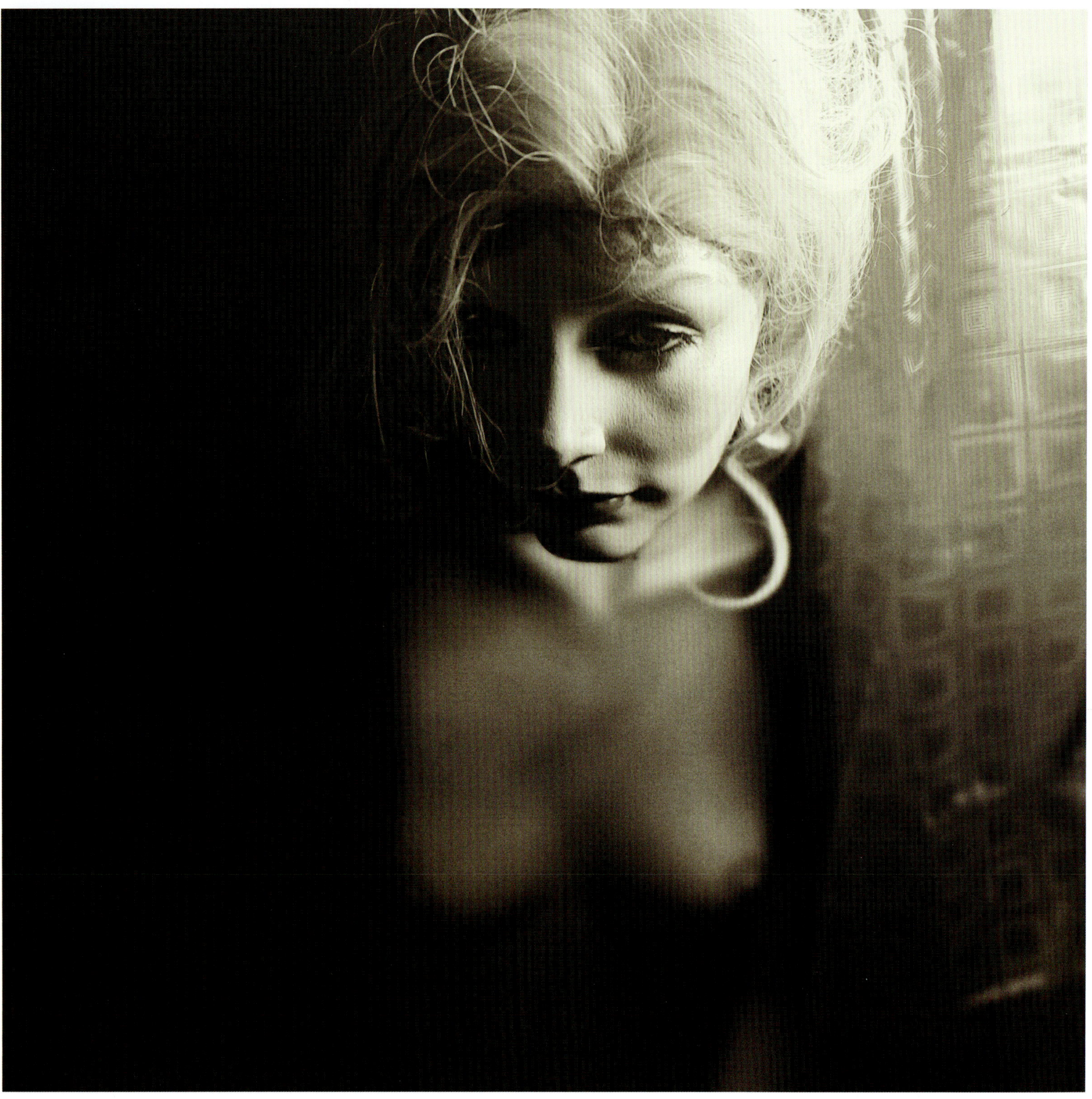

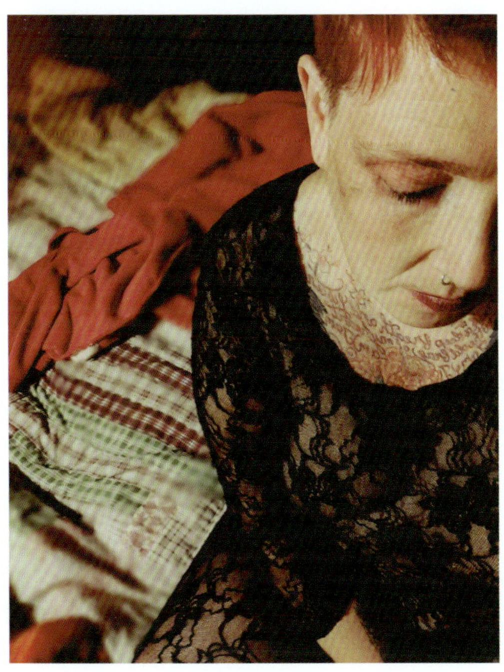

Stages

My body
Thunderous
Naked
Like a heifer
Before the slaughter.

I stand in the middle of the field
Chewing
Chewing
Chewing
And shitting.

I know what's coming.
I see
I feel the darkness.
I feel the weight.
My girth
Solid
Enormous.
I keep my head up.
Waiting.
Chewing
Chewing.
Chewing.

Stages of life.

The stages of a disease.

It chews
It chews
It chews
Thunderous.
You can't clap it out.
You make do.
You have compassion.
You love.
You live.

I stand in the field
A solid mass.
Naked.
Soft eyes
Breathing.
Stars shine above my head.
My enormity shadowed by the night sky.

Stages of life.

Old Dressers

Old dressers
Sold
Lugged up and down steps
Oak
Nice hardware
Open drawers and find wall paper liners
Pencils roll back and forth
With teeth marks
And worn erasers
Travel size soaps
From hotels
A lone handkerchief

I oil the wood
I wax the drawers
I wonder what you were like
What your bedroom looked like
What your face looked like
The sound of your laugh
How your shoulders slumped.

I put the price tag
On your 3 drawer dresser
And I sell it to a family
Who just moved here
Just bought a house in Hancock County
They used to live somewhere else
They have big dreams
The dresser will go into their bedroom
They will fill it
With organic cottons
Silk underthings
Their shoulders do not slump.
They wear LL Bean boots
Wool jackets
Their names aren't old
Like Stanley
Or Basil
Or Pearl

I help carry the dresser out and set it in the
back of their SUV
The pencil
With teeth marks
And a stained handkerchief
Thrown in the wastebasket.

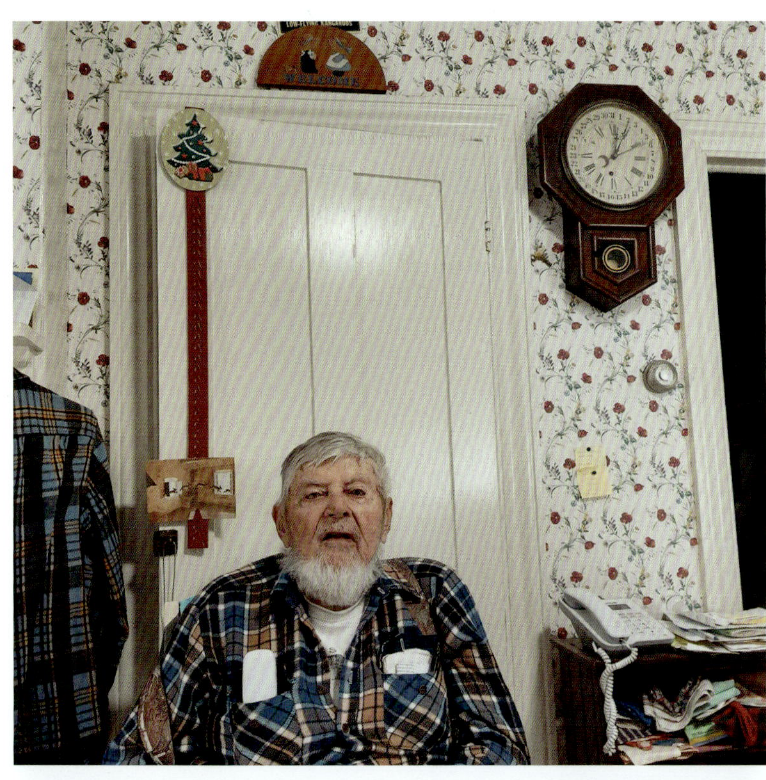

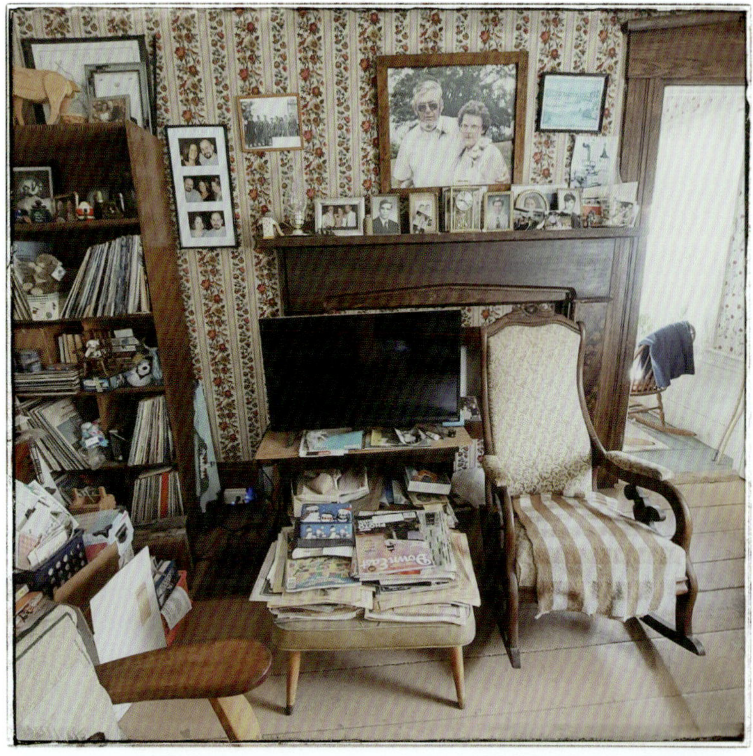

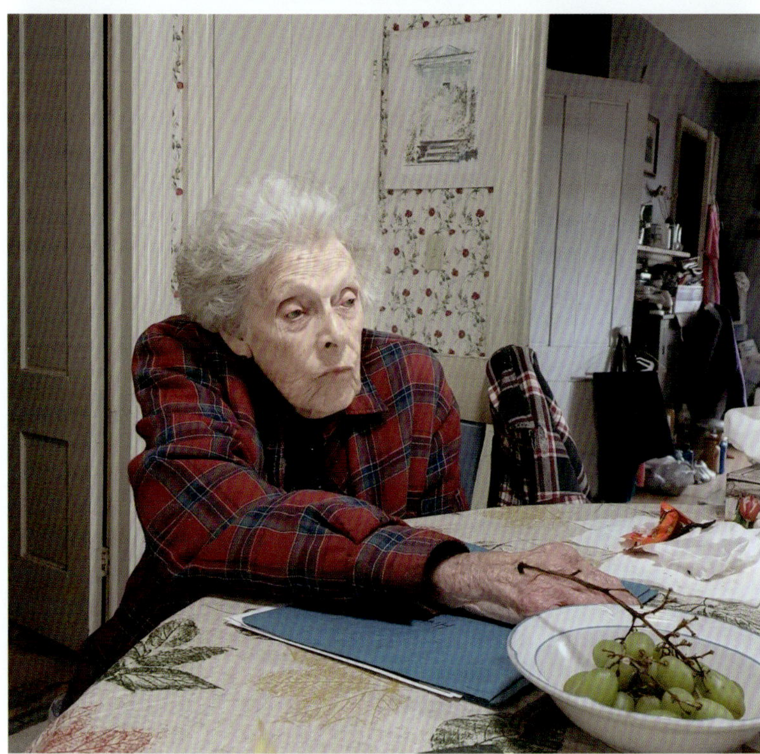

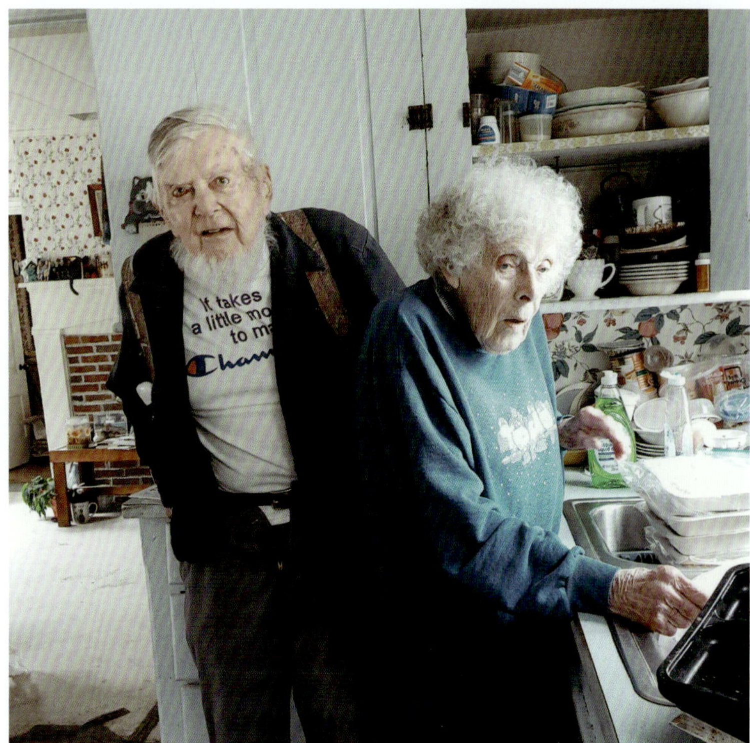

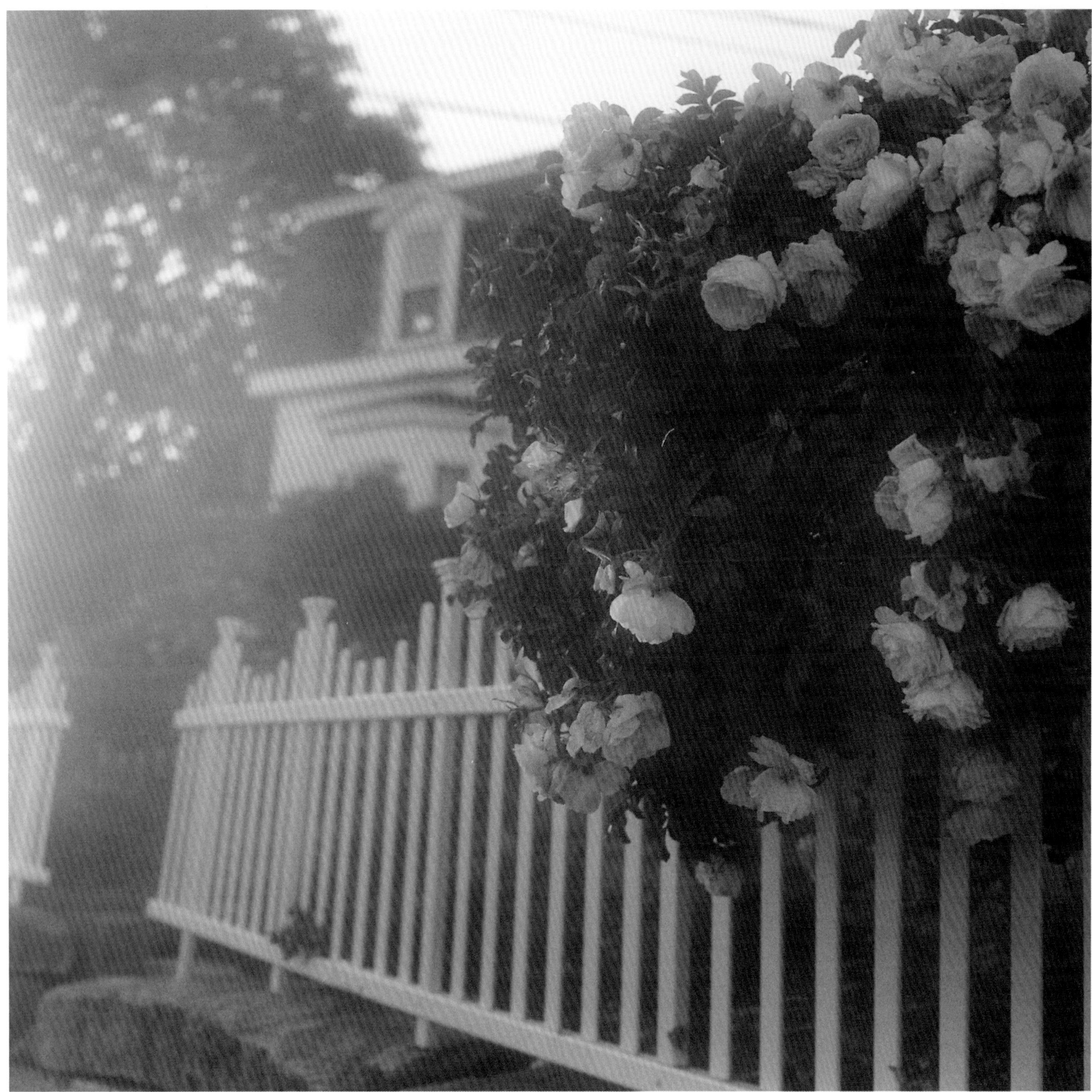

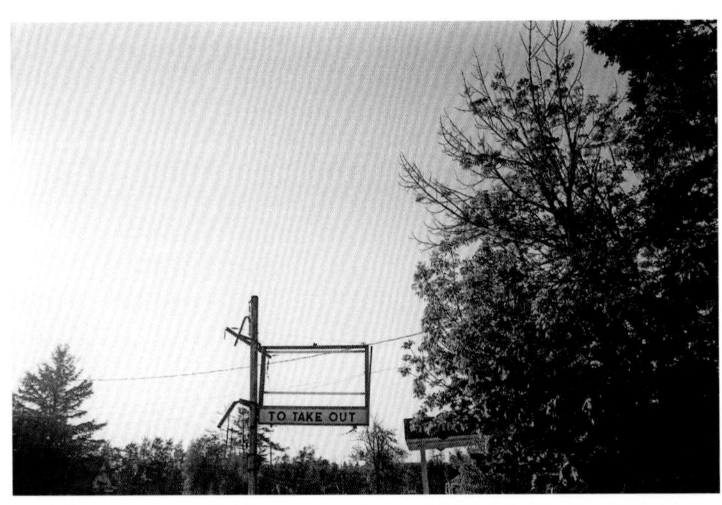
TO TAKE OUT

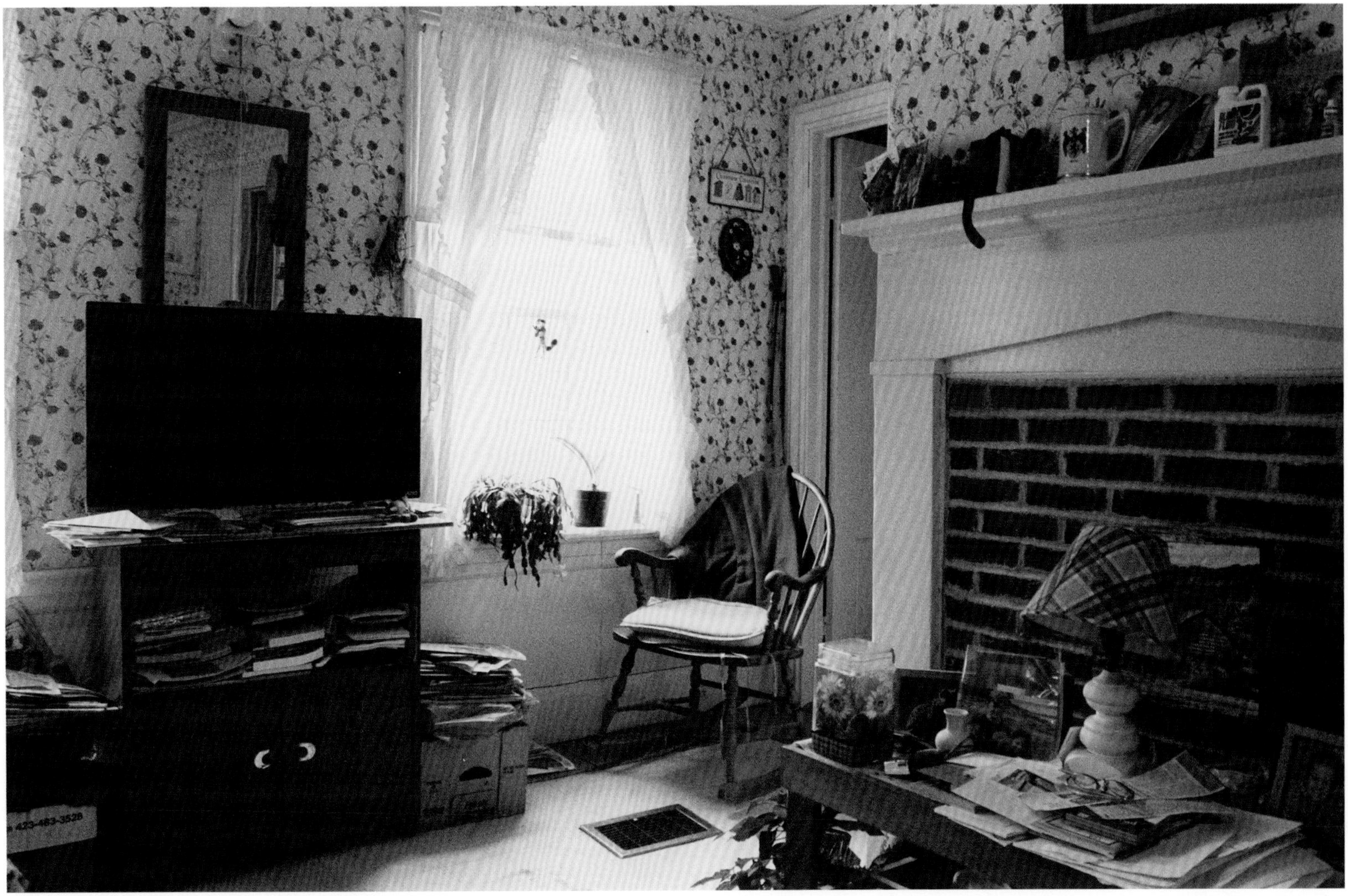

Seen

Most of the time
I do not want
To be SEEN.

I want people to leave me alone.

To not coo or cluck
Rubbing their hands
Up and down my arms
Like a stairway banister
Using me
To climb up

Why is it important
For my work to be seen
For me to be seen
As an artist

Instead of just wacky
Sensitive
Kristie

Oh you know
Kristie
The one with the hair
She's chubby, plump, fat
From Deer Isle
Had a shoe store
Worked at the chocolate store
You know the one!
Yeah!
That's her!
Well now she thinks she's an artist!
Right?
She takes pictures of dolls!
Can you imagine?!
Have you seen them?
CREEPY!
She should take pictures of lobster boats
Lighthouses
Maybe another weird selfie!

But here I am

Wanting to be seen!

People hug me
Asking me what I've been up to
As they stand in a room
With 40 photographs.
I sigh/shrug
Not much.

They walk around the perimeter
Of the show
Of the images
They don't stop
They just slowly stroll
Not even looking

Yeah
Do people buy your doll pictures, Kristie?

I want to answer
But I shrug

Why do you take pictures of dolls, anyway?
Ugh.
And dead animals!
And abandoned houses!
Weird!
I think you'd do better with boats.
Lighthouses!
Babies.
I want to be SEEN.

Rubbing my arm
Up and down
Climbing
I shake you off
And I'm the one who is climbing the stairs
I'm seeing myself
And I love her
In a way that is foreign and familiar
The best is yet to come.

Love,
You know
Kristie
The one with the hair!
The doll photographer.
She's fat
But nice.

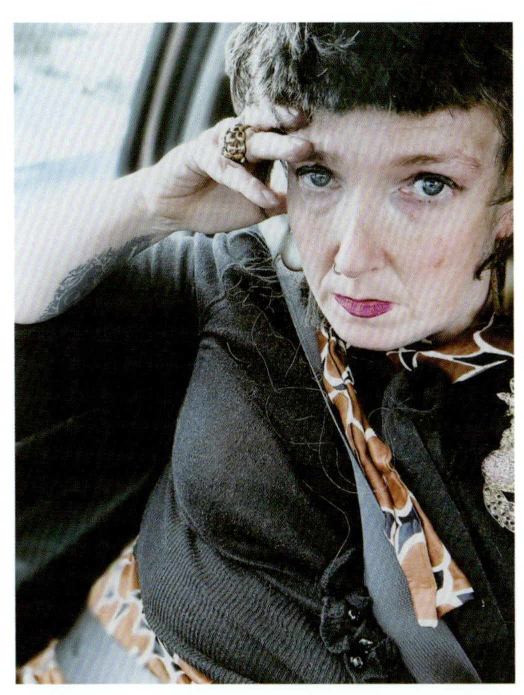

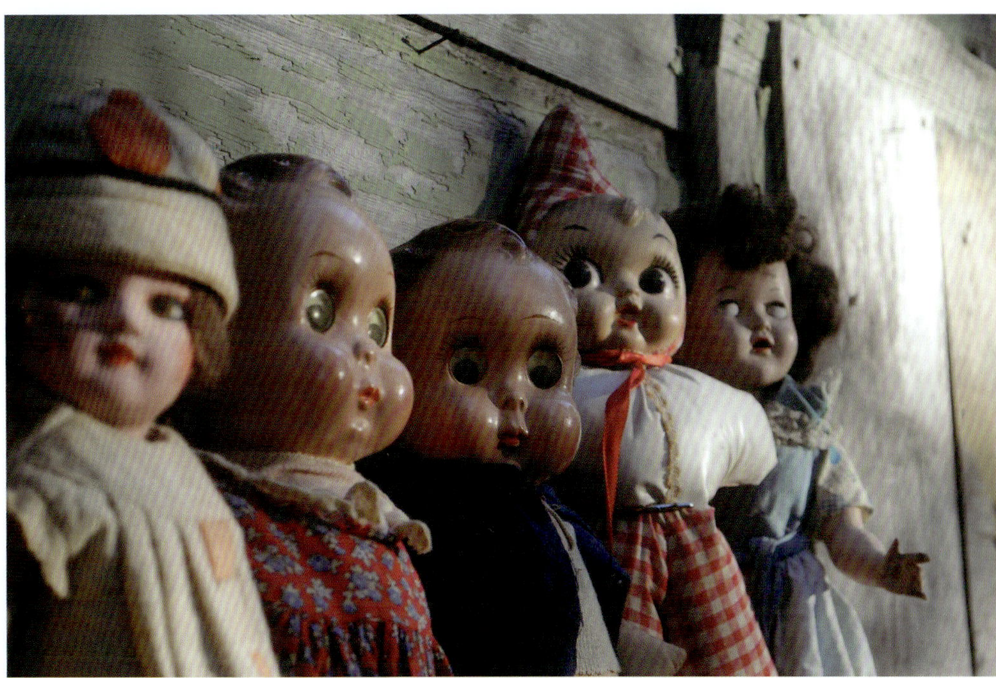

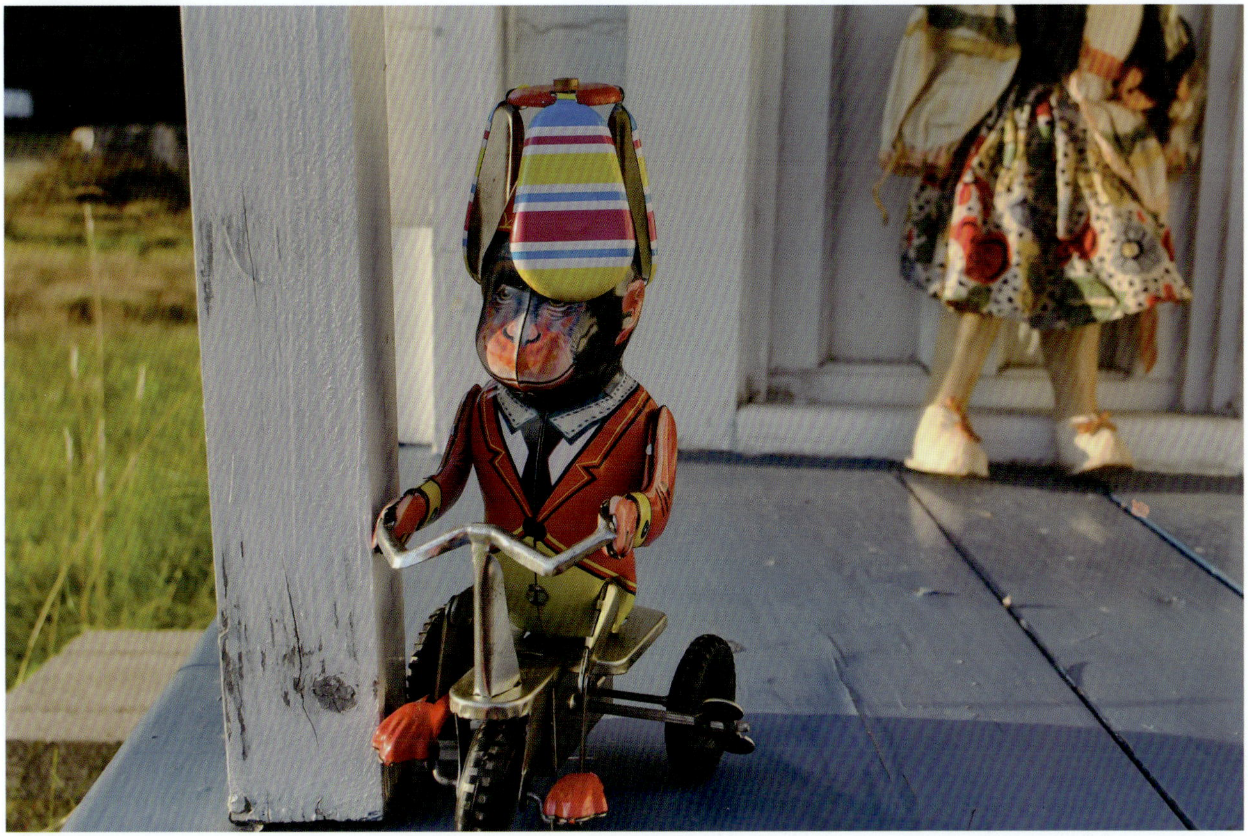

Meatball

Feeling blue?
Feeling UGHHH?
Here's some comic relief!

I bought a vintage silk dress recently. Great. Who cares. I knew, if it fit me, it would be SNUG. I tried it on the day I bought it and was like uh NOPE. This morning I was like FFFFF IT. Let's try again. I'll wear it under a skirt. So, I'm a perimenopausal gal, right? Sure. I'm already a voluptuous lady of fire. I pull the dress over my head. Fine. My head fits. My neck fits. My boobs? Squashed. Belly? Owww! The worst are my hips. Sweet JESUS!
AND then a Miracle HAPPENED.
A CHRISTMAS MIRACLE.
(OR SOLSTICE.)
The animals of the world and all the GODS said this poor woman looks like a pickled sausage. Let's help her.
The seam burst!
There was light!
There was relief!
There was flesh!
And, I laughed and laughed.
It was a glorious gift. The Dress was meant to be worn as a Blouse.
Feel better? You should!
Eat that fudge. Cookie cookie.
Lots of Love from your favorite Hot Flash Queen,
Kristie
Xoxoxo
Your favorite MEATBALL.

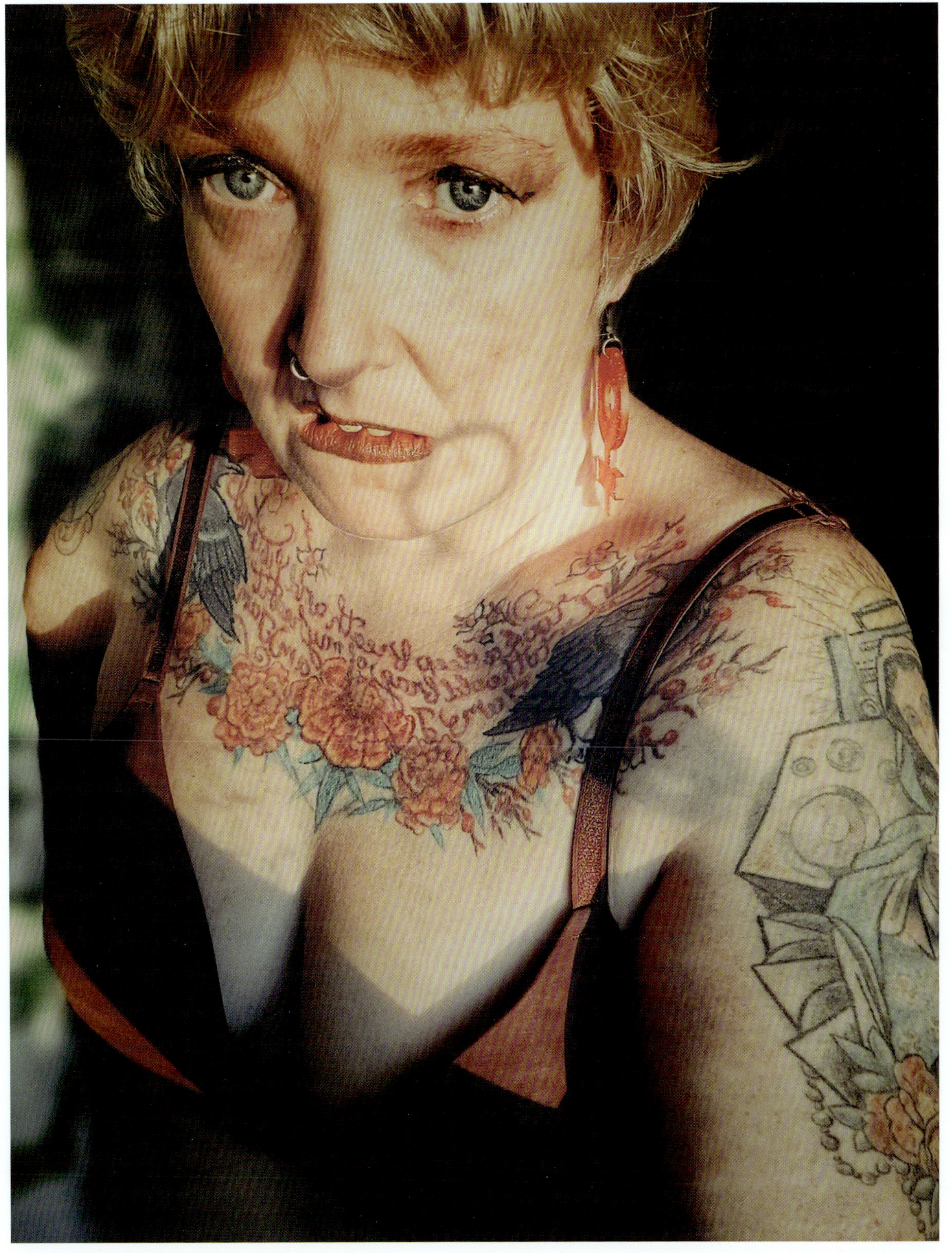

Dead Stock

Dead stock
Vintage but new with tags
Who else gets excited
To see an old dress from Sears?
What medium size Lady just passed away?
Did she have a perm?
I like her style.
Lots of button down dresses
With wide skirts
Polka dots
And plaid.
Oh!
My kind of lady!
Faux pearl buttons,
Pleats,
Stone washed denim.

Oh I wish you and I could go for a ride in your big Oldsmobile.
Somehow I imagine her in a big car.
Maybe drinking a Tab,
An iced tea.

Did she have cats like me,
Or a nice golden retriever?
Or a schnauzer?
Did she like Krackle candy bars?
Mr. Goodbar?
I imagine her hair brown.
Not short short
But certainly not long.
She wore clip earrings
And had a cool keychain.
Did this lady wear glasses like me?
Why didn't she like these Gitano elastic waist pleated tapered pants?
Did she regret buying them in the color of putty?
Why do I want to buy them when I'm not a size 7,
And I think the color is hideous?
I wonder if she left things in her pockets like I always do?
Gum, screws, safety pins, a couple bucks, bobby pins.
An occasional earring,
A receipt,
A beer bottle cap.

Who was this woman?
New with tags.
Dead stock.
Why didn't she wear her clothes?
And did she die of covid?
Cancer?
Or did she just move into assisted living?
Her dumb kids just dropped off garbage bags labeled
"Mom's crap."
Or was she just echoing what I hear all day long,
"I'm just downsizing!"

I fondle, lovingly, an Oshkosh women's dress that was never worn.
What was her name?
Rose?
Janet?
Mary?
Barbara?
It's killing me.
I look through the racks of clothing
Hoping to find clues
A tag with your name on it?
Nope.
These clothes did not hang in the closet of a nursing home.
They hung in your closet.
Did you gain a bunch of weight
Like me?
Did you watch Dallas?
Dynasty?
Falcon Crest?
Now your clothes hang on overcrowded racks in Goodwill.
Smooshed in with ugly clothes from Walmart in cheap polyester.
Your clothes are the most exciting things in this entire store.

Dead stock.
Vintage but new with tags
Discolored from age.
Beige dresses never worn
No breasts
No hips to fill them out.
No missing buttons.
They just hang
With a colored barb hanging from the cuff indicating the price.

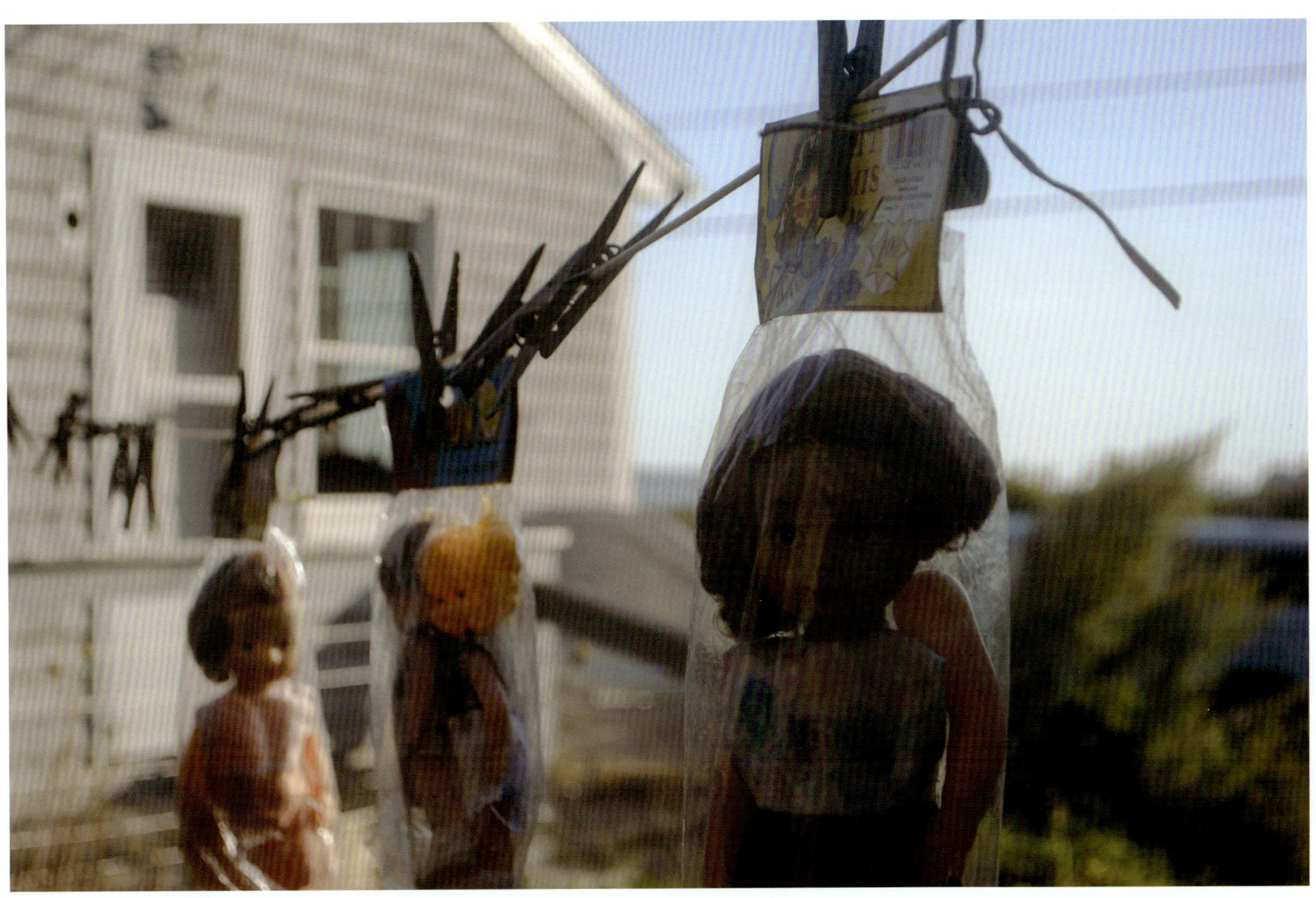

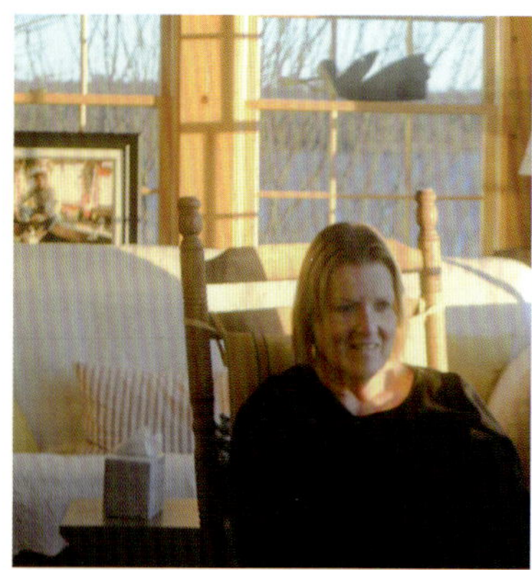

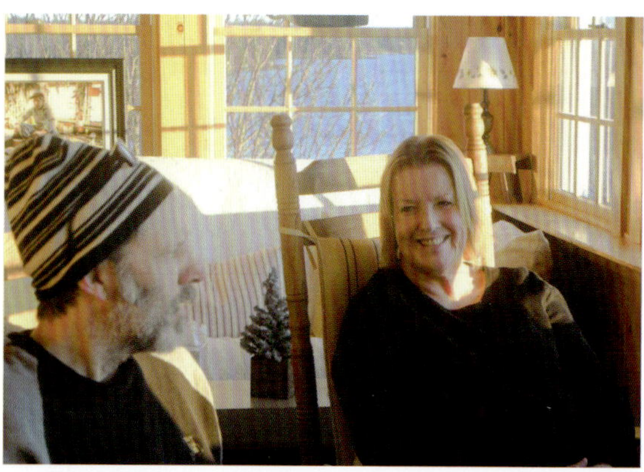

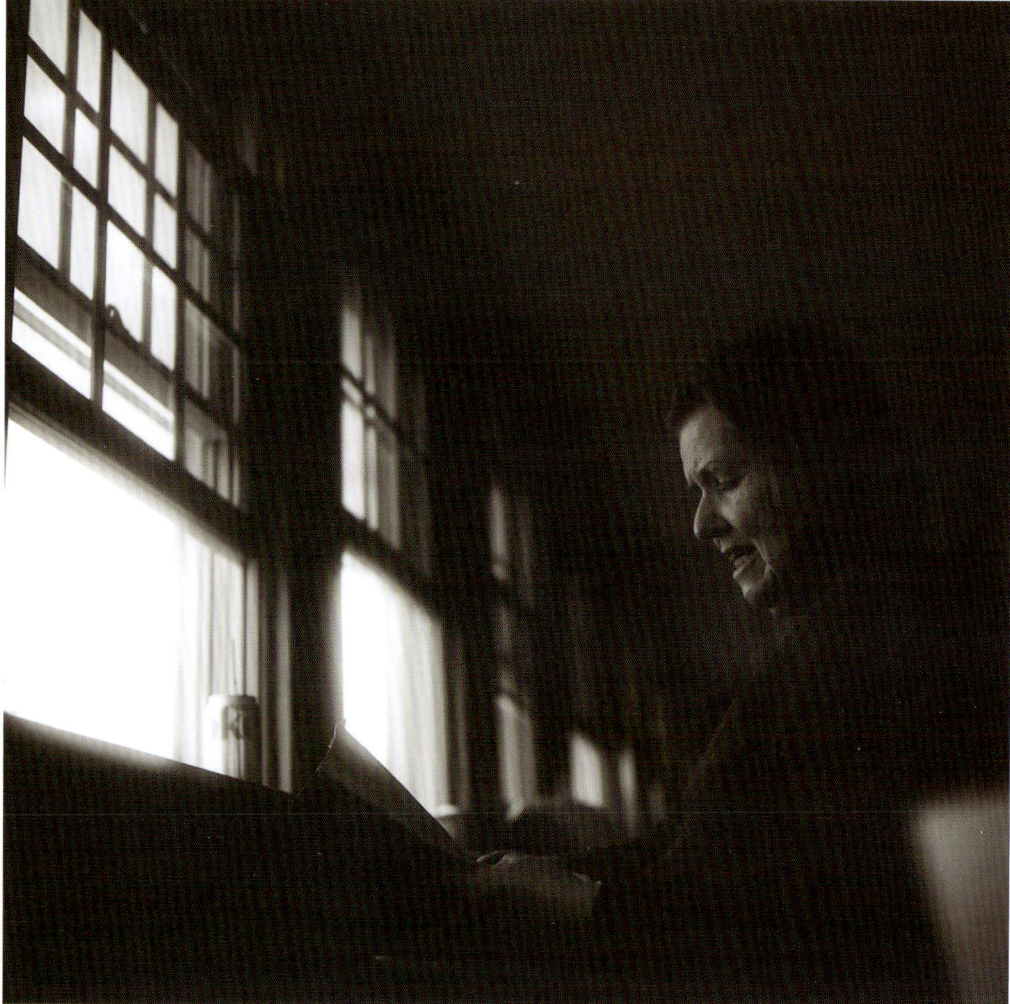

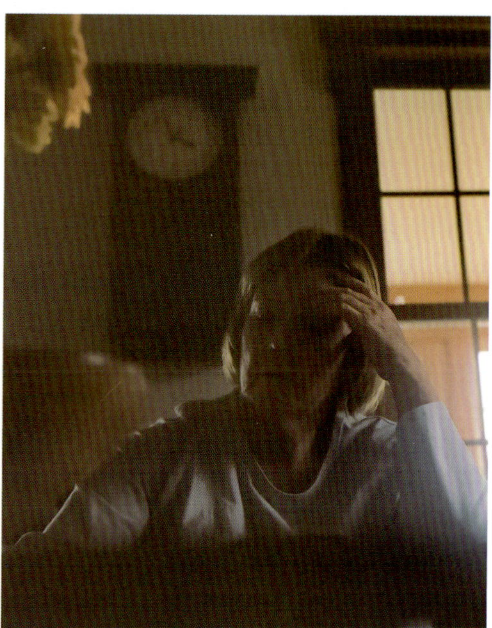

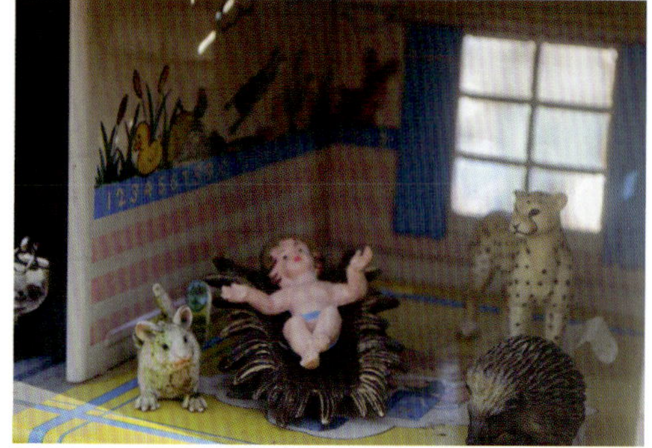

Evaluation

Kristie,
What do you hope to get out of this
appointment today?
I begin,
A long ramble
But I do answer.
I want to know where we are in this disease
And what to expect.
What I can do to help
My Mom
And myself
For the stages of this difficult road we are
on.

The social worker commends me
Applauds me
On how supportive and intuitive I am
Asked me if I had training.
I laugh.

I tell her as hard it feels right now
I know that it is going to get much much
worse and I want to be equipped with
knowing how to navigate and make sure I
am present with my Mom and her needs.
And for me to feel supported also.

What I don't tell her
Is that I'm exhausted.
I do tell her I have a great husband,
A great doctor,
That I'm on Zoloft.
That I have a few incredibly supportive
friends.
That I have a fantastic Nana
And an aunt who has given me great advice.
I don't tell her that I'm worried
That I'll fail my Mom.
I don't tell her that I'm worried that I'll end
up with this disease too.

I do tell her
I had hoped to travel
I give her the slightest smile.
I look up
And start to cry.
She shakes the tissue box.
I nod.

I don't tell her
That I can't finish this poem
Because even writing the words
Feels too hard.
So I will vacuum
I'll do laundry
And get ready to attend an art reception
My art will hang
I will too
Splayed out
Hammered
And screwed
With stretchmarks and training wheels
Glitter and Googly Eyes
Discolored teeth and chewed fingernails.
"OH hi.
Yeah. That's my photograph. It's Jesus.
And a Cheetah. See?"
I shrug.
I roll my eyes.
Yeah.

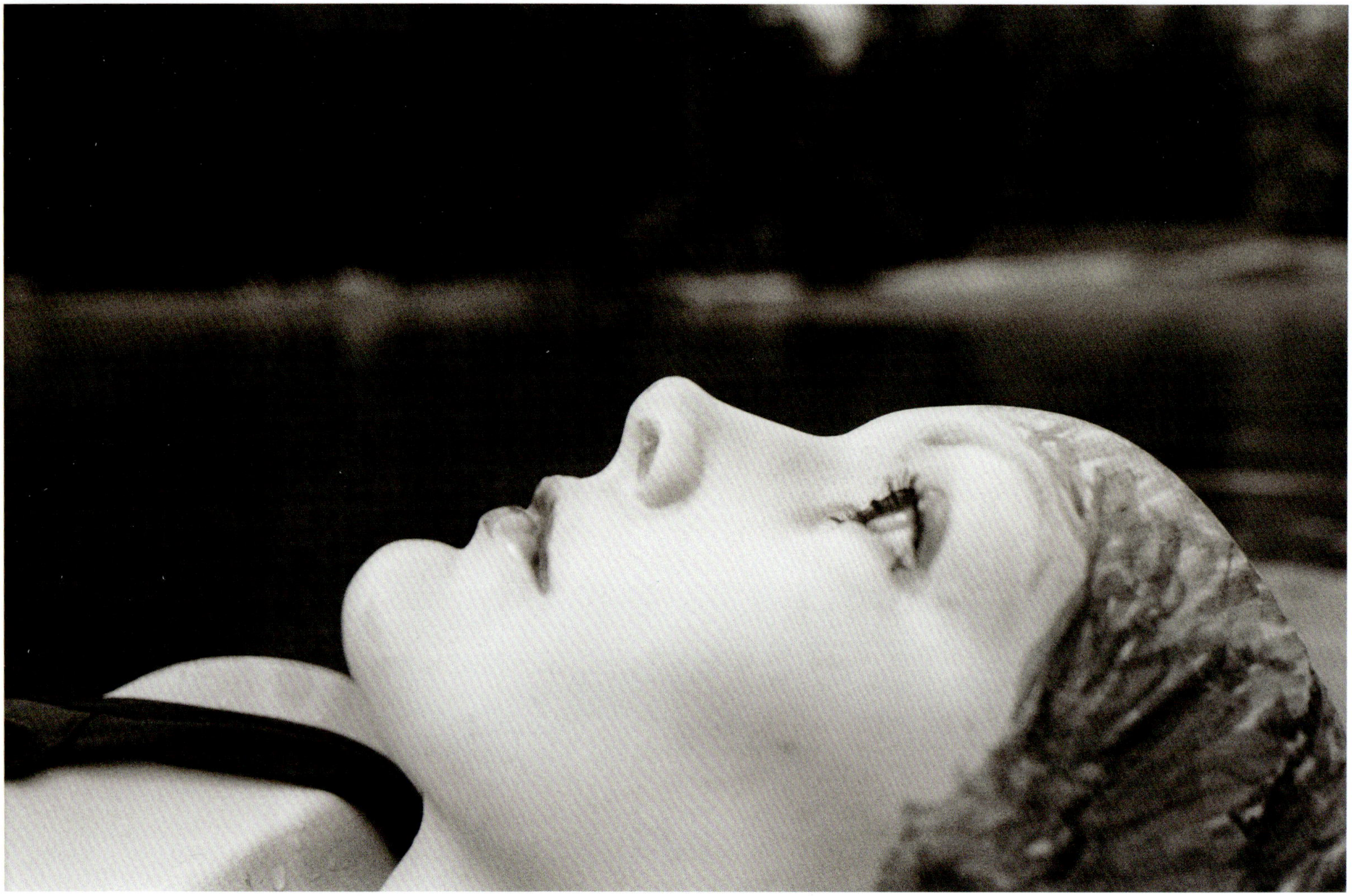

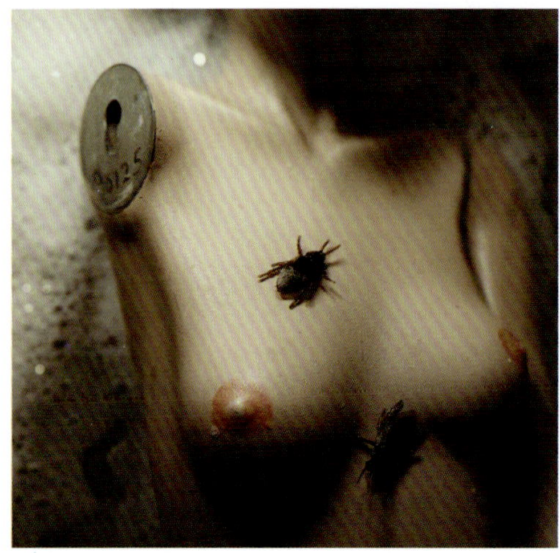

Red Bathrobe

Red bathrobe
With plastic cockroaches
In the left pocket
Plastic red lips
A whistle!
In the right pocket
A doll house miniature telephone.
Anger pours out from every angle
Of the stained red bathrobe.
Stubby hairy legs
Poke out from the hem
Of the red robe.
Medium-sized feet
In black slippers.
Shuffle
Anger
Beer
Insomnia
Night sweats
Cut crystal rocks glass.
The dishes soak
In Palmolive
Or Ajax
There's no Madge.
There's just me.
And I have too much on my brown and white Transfer plate
Potato
Greens
Haddock
Dish pan hands
"You're soaking in it!"
Sundowning syndrome
Shuffling
Agitation
Acute
I'm not the therapist in the family
But I'm the most empathetic. I roll back and forth
A dinghy
I need to be bailed out.
I'm angry!
Plastic cockroaches In my pocket
And a nearly empty beer
I need my plastic lips
A mask.
Isn't that what you all want?
Crazy kooky fun Kristie!
So brave!
Look at her!
You don't wanna know the real me.
I'm too intense
Too scary
I don't want you anywhere near me I'll take the plastic cockroaches
And put them all in my mouth
My phone is off the hook
"You're soaking in it!"

Grocery

At the grocery store with my mom
Up down up looking
We look at cat food cans
Lots of them
She studies them
Asking me if I think Grace would like
tender beef in gravy. "Let's try it!"
I show her a can of chicken, sliced.
She nods.
I grab 4 and throw them into her cart.
We look at bananas.
We look at lettuce.
We hold apples
And decide they feel mealy.
I lug, tug
At gallon jugs of water.
I have her shopping lists.
Most of this stuff she doesn't need.
What I mean is she already has it.
Many of said items.
Sometimes, I tell her no.
I place my hand on her back
And say, "You already have that."
Sometimes, she answers,
"Yes, Mother."
Sometimes, I just put the item back.
Or just take it out of her cart.
Leaving it on some shelf.
In the grocery store
I always see people I know.
So does she.
But she doesn't remember them.
Today
I see a woman
I know
And she looks at me,
And at my Ma,
Who is still looking at cat food.
She asks me how I am.
She asks me if I need help.
Yes, yes, yes, I do.
I don't say that.
I say yeah.
She offers to help.
But she's going into busy season...
I immediately know I won't ask her for
help.
I thank her and tell her I'll be in touch.
My Ma and I go down another aisle
Looking at soap.
I tease her,
Gently,
Asking if she wants the anti stress soap.
We look at toothbrushes.
Soft
Medium
Green
Blue
Pink.
No decision can be made.
"Kristie! You're such a great daughter!"
My Mom tells people that she doesn't
remember, "I'm so blessed to have Kris. I
don't know what I'd without her."
I roll my eyes.
And say. "Ready Freddy?"
"Ready Freddy."
I load the groceries in her truck
That she can no longer drive herself.
We go to another store.
And, now that it's spring, we go get her a
soft-serve vanilla ice cream cone.
I drive,
Looking for Deer,
I am looking for things to distract her.
And give us both pause, a reason to smile.

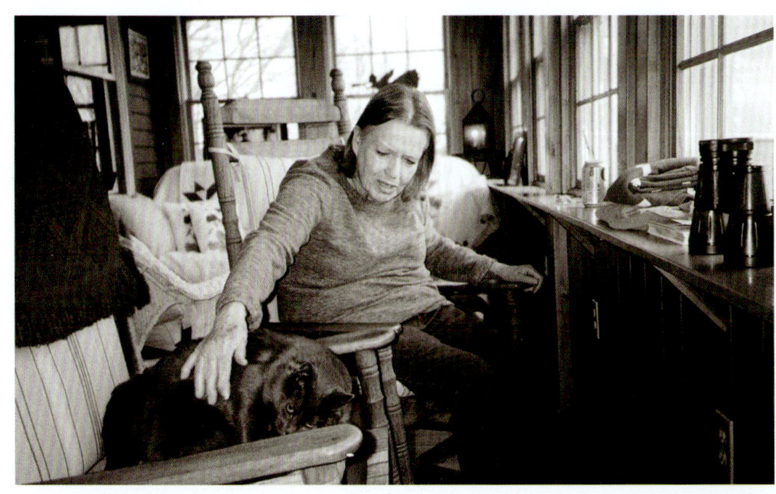

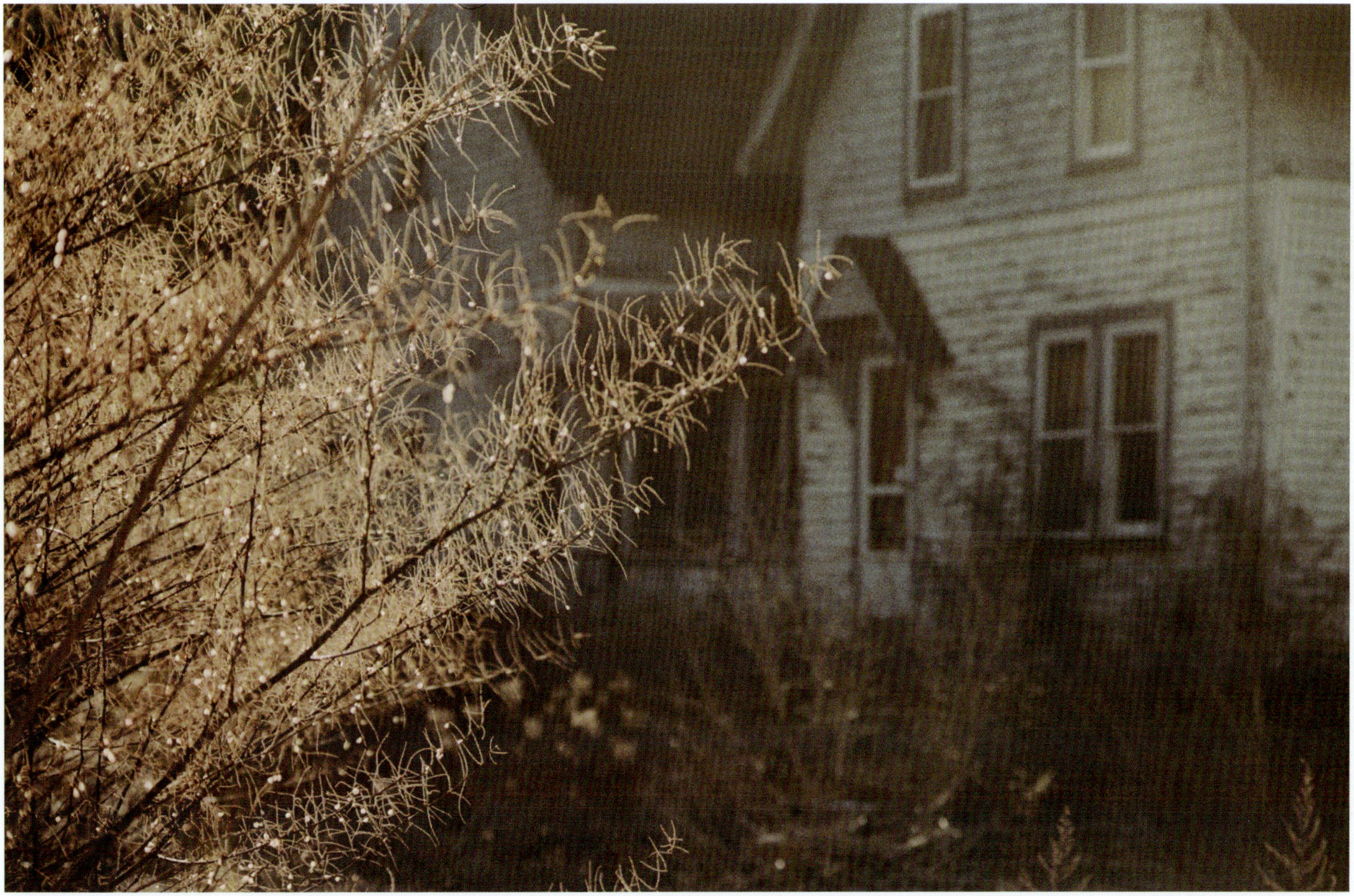

Forget Me Not

Forget me not
Remember when we used to go on car rides
Just to go
To get out.
We'd circle the Island
Criss crossing back down familiar roads
With ponds, ocean views, fields of black
eyed susans, And a sea of golden rod and
queen anne's lace.
Deer would be under apple trees
Occasionally flicking their white tails.
We would slow to a crawl
Roll down windows
Call out to them our protection song.
"BE CAREFUL..."
I am not even sure of my own footing.
I never seem to pick my feet up.
A stumbling shuffle.
I really am dreading this ride.
Criss crossing
Going down roads that are tough to handle
Making you question can I make it back in
one piece?
It seems like all I see are white deer tails
flicking CAUTION
CAUTION
I am driving white knuckled
Turning the music down lower,
The need to focus on what may be just up
ahead.
Black eyed susans
Damp with rain
A perpetual fog
Repetition
Repetition
Repetition
The drizzle over the fields
The windshield wipers barely making much
difference Fogged in.
I need to start having difficult
conversations.
It is always harder for me going down a
mountain than up. I need to document
wishes, stories, and prescriptions.
I need to photograph you.

I feel guilty that I am thinking about myself.
I just worry I am not strong enough
To enter this white out blizzard with you
And see you through with kindness and
protection.
My husband tells me I can.
I will bring you flowers, food, and
protection.
I will have hard conversations.
I will hold your hand.
We'll drive around the back roads
With flecks of Indian paintbrushes, daisies,
and wild roses. I'll be gentle.
Forget me not.

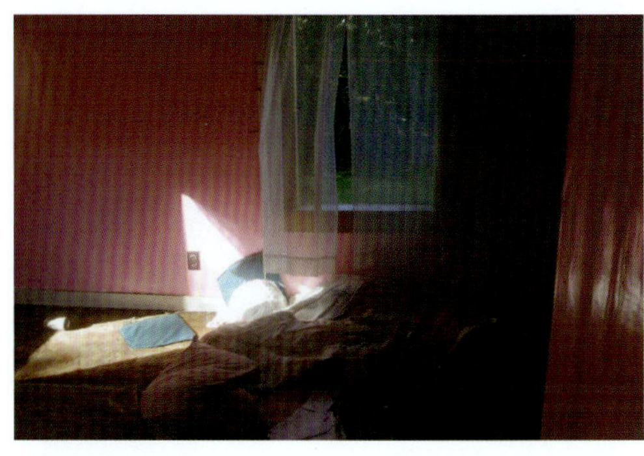

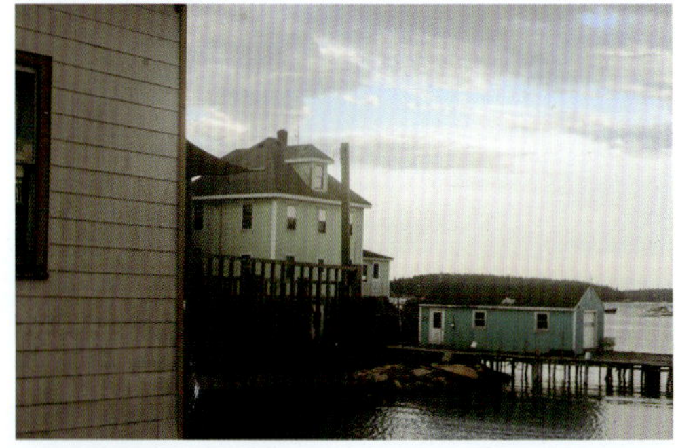

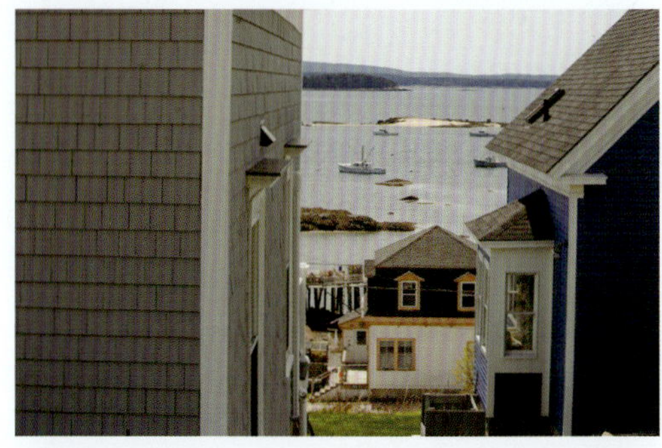

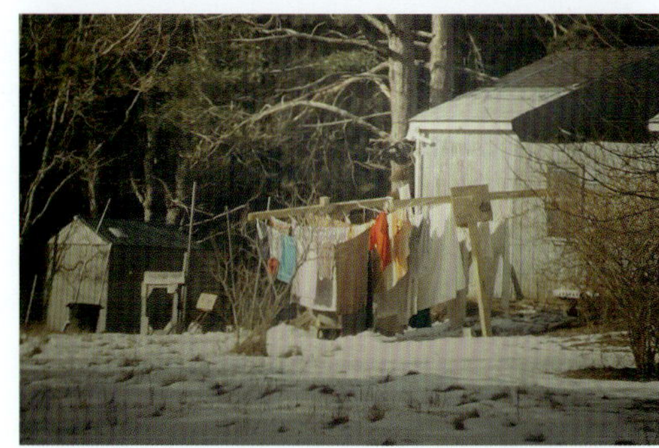

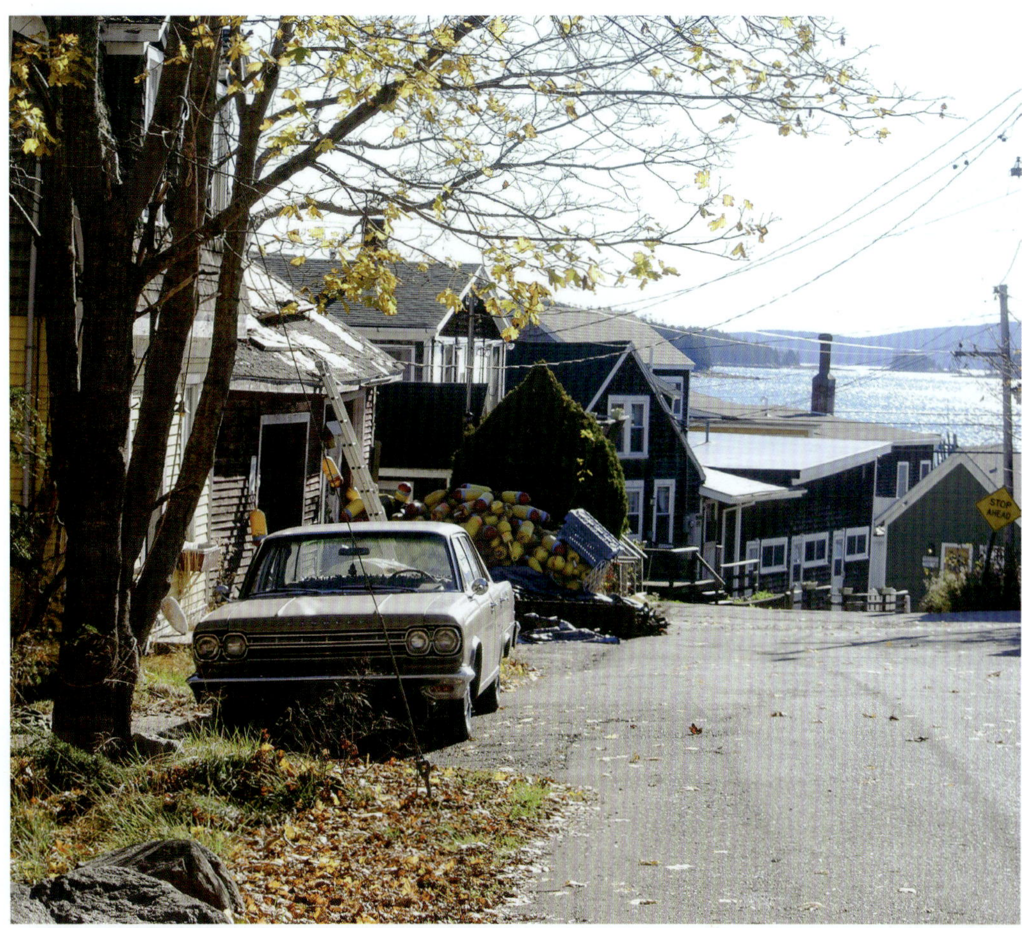
STOP
AHEAD

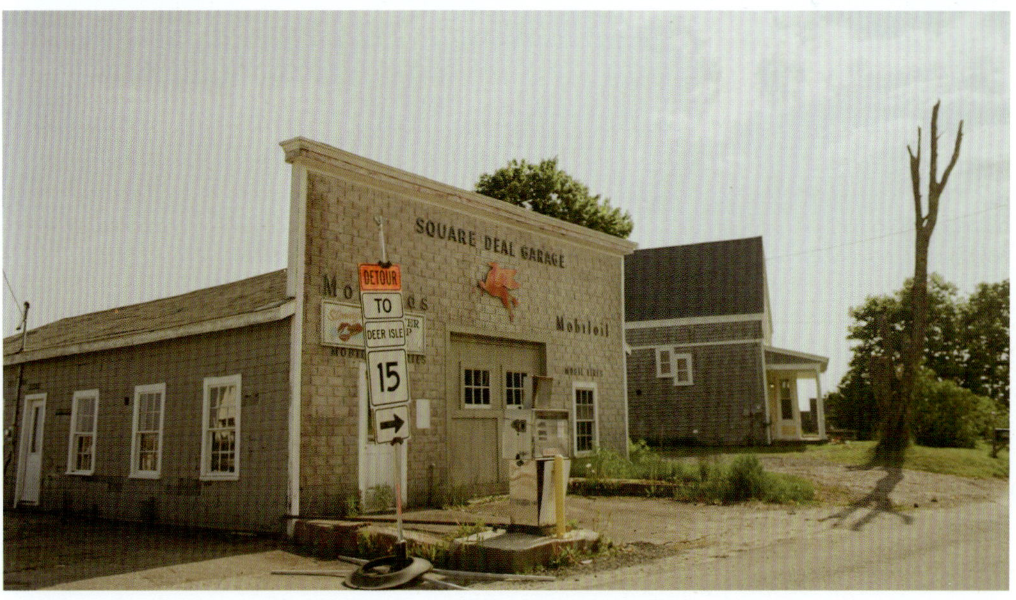
SQUARE DEAL GARAGE
DETOUR
TO
DEER ISLE
15
Mobiloil

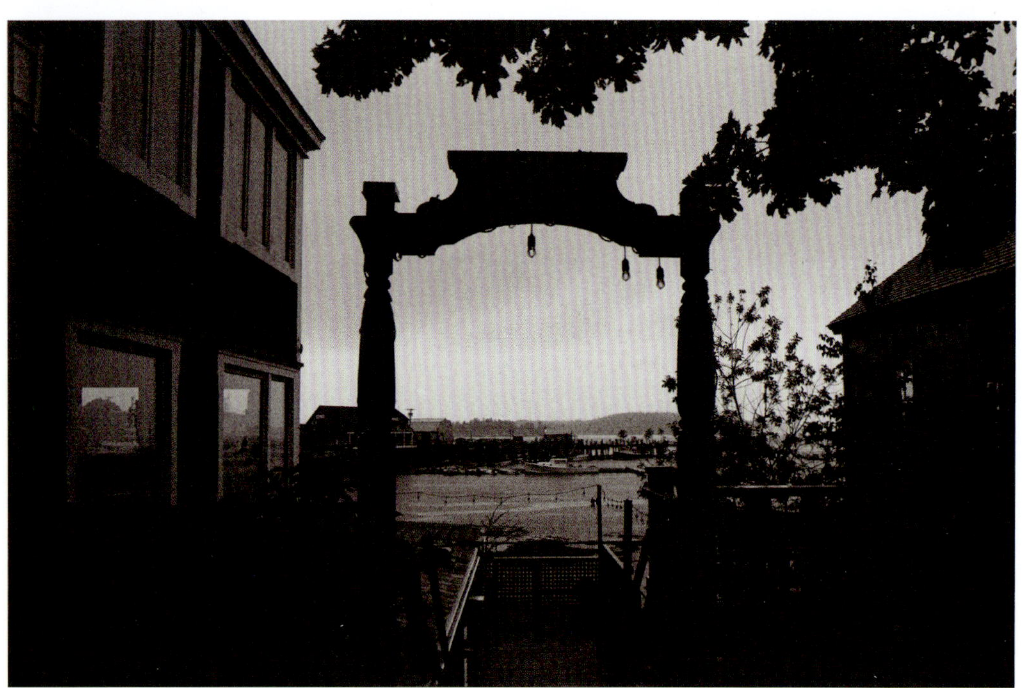

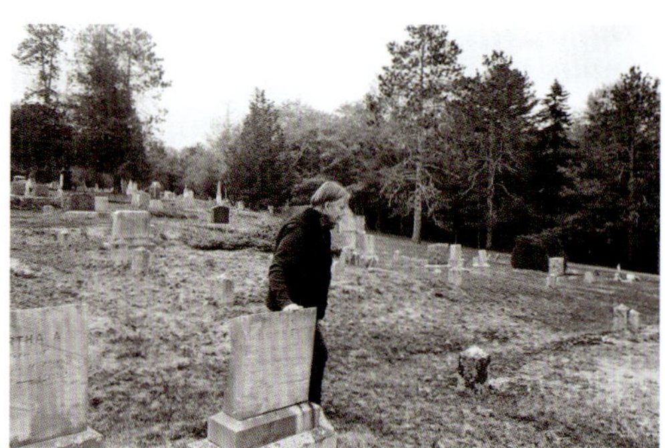

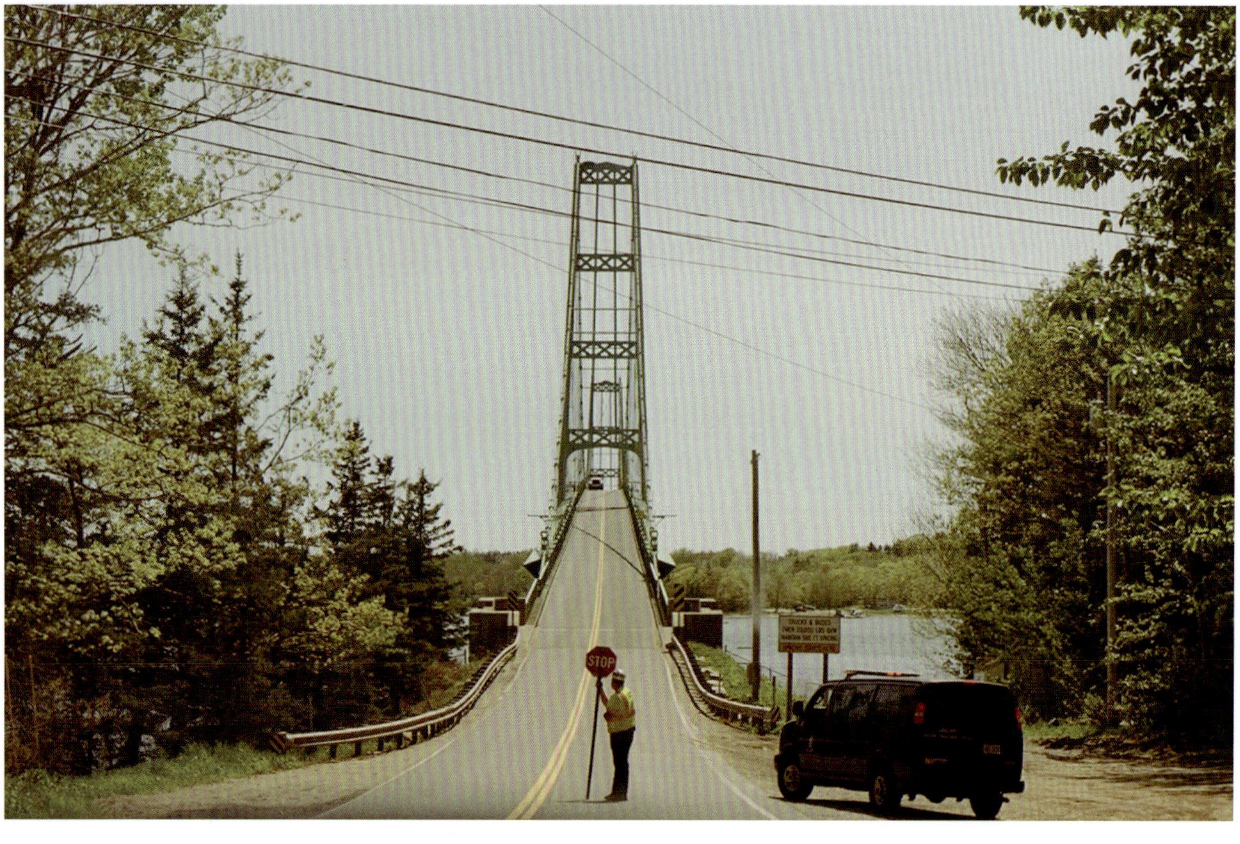

I'm Failing

I'm failing
You
And me.

I want to help you
Not bully you.

I wish I could be tough.

I try to act, to you, that I'm okay
That this isn't a big deal.
But it is.
I want the best for you.

It is a relatively new role for me
To be a parent.
To try to be supportive
Yet make sure things get done.
To balance things out.

I wonder what Honk would say.
I know what his Mother thinks.
I think I can imagine what Holly would say.

I just have to keep trying
To be gentle
To hold your hand
To make phone calls
Go to appointments
To see doctors,
Bankers,
Lawyers,
All smiling behind a mask and looking at
you with love.
Trying not to show my anxiety
And my worry
That i am not strong enough
To do this
To be the best daughter
For you.

I wonder if it is normal
To have my mind race night after night
I dodged my doctor appointment this week.

Sometimes facing things is hard
It must run in our family
You blamed the icy driveway
I don't want you to fall
I offer to come get you
To borrow my husbands car.
You decline
I bite my tongue
Not wanting to scold
I, too, didn't want to face my doctor
Literally
And tell her the meds aren't working
I'm stressed
I'm not sleeping
I rescheduled.
And I'll reschedule your appointment too,
Mom.
We have to do this.

I wish I was tough.
I wish I wasn't failing.

Middle Aged Woman

More and more this happens;
I pause
I stop
Where did this come from?
A new obstacle.
And this too...
Where did I put that?
Late yesterday at a tax office
Rummaging and rummaging through
My fake Gucci wallet
Trying to find my id
Just gift cards and receipts.
Feeling,
And looking,
Old.

Where did that fat roll come from?
I have to laugh.
Really?
It came from chips.
It came from cookies.
It came from stress.

Where did all these wrinkles and
discolorations come from?
I kick rocks in front of me
As I walk down streets.
Nothing is ever ironed out.
Nothing in my life has been smooth sailing.
What did I expect?

Where did I put that bill?
Why is my car rusting out?
Here I am
Pushing 50
And I've done this and that
But I can't even make up my mind about
what haircut I want.

Why is it on other people
I see age
And it is beautiful?
On me it looks like another bruised fruit
Not even good enough to make banana
bread with,
Or apple sauce.
Just straight to the compost.

Maybe that's it?
I have never felt the YEAH YEAH OH
YEAH
ME thing.
I've picked at myself
Hard.
So much that I've bled.
I've got scars,
I've got fat.
The rust.
Infinite dust.
But I'm still kicking rocks down the street
As I walk
Singing to myself.
A giggle here and there.

People tell me the reason why they like me
Is that I'm real.
Yeah.
I'm real.
Like the bill that you forgot to pay.
The lie that you casually tell.
The bra that doesn't quite fit.
I dig in.
I'm non-threatening to most people
Because I don't bother covering up my
faults and flaws.
There simply aren't enough creams and
concealers.
Go for the fiberglass bondo.
Smooth sailing?
Pffttt.
That's for losers!
Smudged lipstick,
Chewed nails,
But a belly full of laughter.
My body is like a fluffanutter sandwich,
To hell with it!

I don't put the bra on.
I roll my eyes at myself.
You can't be too serious.
I am a middle aged woman.
I am salty, sassy, and I know when to shut
up and just listen.
Time to move my fat ass in corduroys.
Swish swish swish.
God, Where is my phone?
Where did I put my coffee?
I have to laugh.

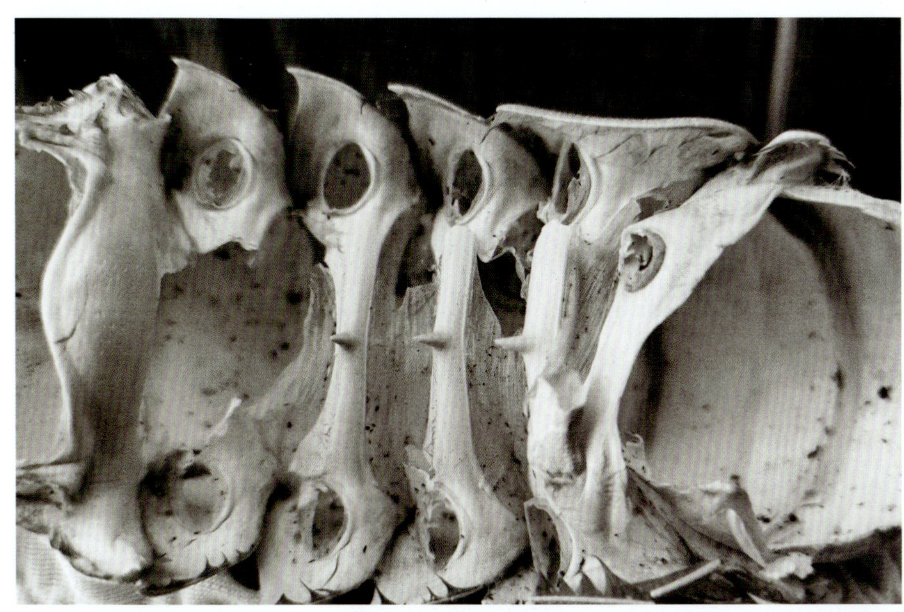

I close my eyes.
Breathing.
Breathing.

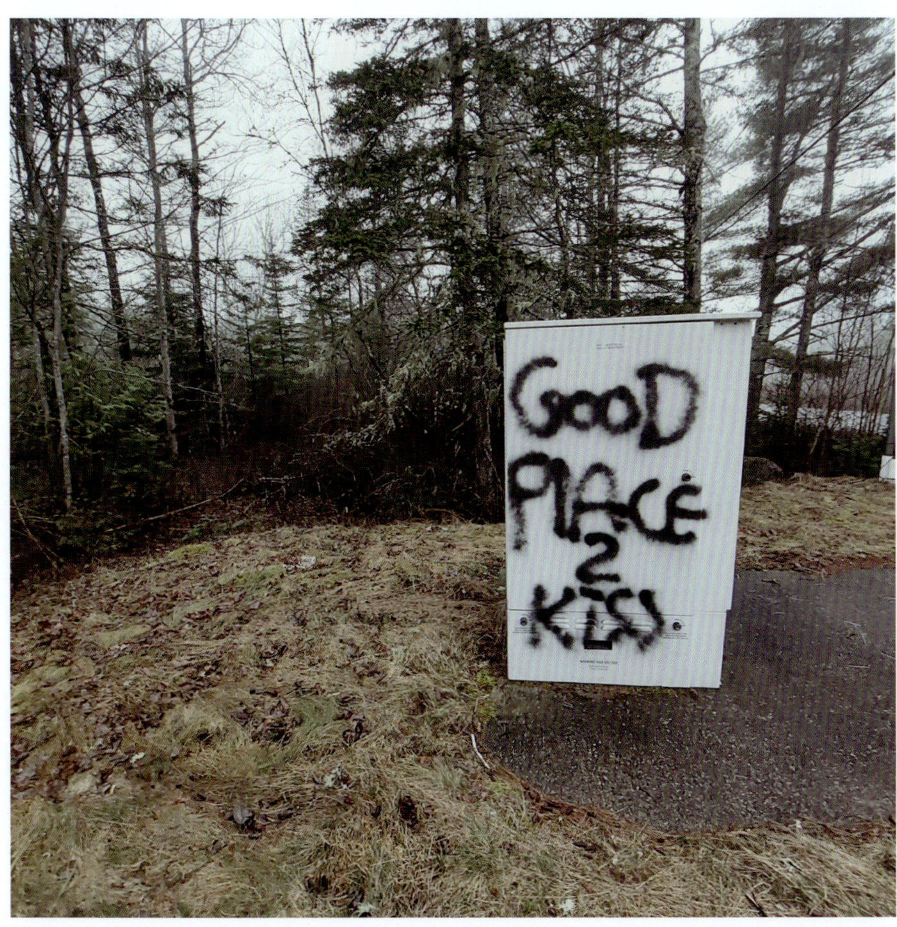

A New Carwash

A new car wash opened
A few blocks away
We already had a bunch of car washes
But I guess someone thought we needed
another. At the top of my street
A gas station/convenience store
Buy your gas,milk,beer,scratch tickets.
They sell pre-made sandwiches
Pizza too.
Chunks of ice.
People smoke cigarettes
Near the prefab picnic tables.
At the bottom of my dead end street
Is a brewery
With a beer garden
Live music sometimes
Pizza too.
Sometimes I think about going there.
On occasion I do, like twice a year.
I just would rather not.
Up the street and around the corner
Is a pet store.
I go there more than 2x a year.
I buy our cats their flea medicine there
And sometimes treats.
I talk to the birds,the lizards, the fish.
I wonder what they are thinking of being in
captivity. Are they bored?
The lights,the peering blurred faces,
the noise.
I work a couple blocks from my house.
It is nice to be able to walk to work
Without driving half an hour or more.
My husband works 4 or 5 blocks from home.
We are townies.
I've lived in this town for almost 17 years
now. I've been back in this area for 21 years.
The one thing I notice is more people.
More people are moving here.

Sometimes I wonder why.
Why here
Sure, it is beautiful.
But how do they all make a living?
They don't look like customer service or
food workers.
My husband wants to retire.
Me?
I have no idea.
I'm just tired.
My bones are tired.
My car is tired.
Leaking oil
And rattling.
Our house is tired.
Down to the foundation.
Build another car wash.
Another restaurant that is just meh
People will come
Wanting premium.
I like resting in my lawn chair
In my backyard
Looking up at the sky
Making shapes out of the clouds
The same way I did as a girl.
I watch my cats get the zoomies
And make lists in my head.
Things I have to do.
I drink my coffee out of a green pottery
mug
I'm happy that no one is calling my name.
The birds seem happy
Some clothes on the line that I forgot to
take in.
I close my eyes.
Breathing.
Breathing.
The trees shadows move across my face.
The clouds morph into different shapes
My cats run up trees
I smile
Quietly
Looking at my chipped pink toe nail polish.
Picking up the green mug
Grateful

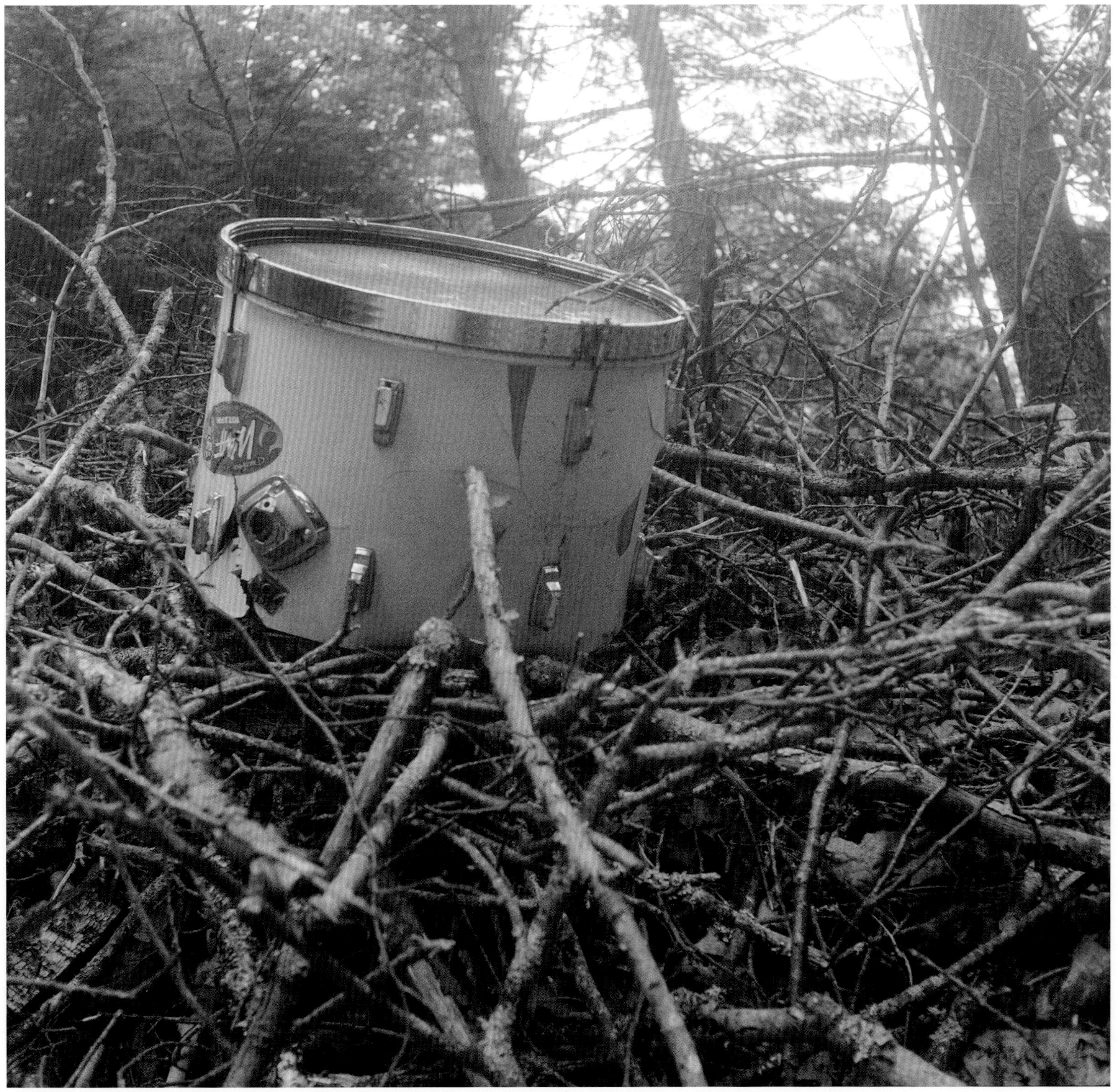

I catch my reflection

I catch my reflection
In windows
Of shops
Of old houses
With Squirrels living in their walls
I see this woman
With a face made of birch bark
I see turkey vultures hover over me I see a mouth
Pinched
Rugosa red
A tight bow
I see long earrings
Hang from pink ears
That look like rosemary
Lavender
Thyme
I catch my face
In cold mirrors
I'm out of focus
Distracted
Squirrels run
Over my medium sized
Wide feet.
I'm not a willow tree
I'm not walnut
Or cherry
I'm a pine tree
With splinters
And bark
Crows feet March
All around sad eyes
I'm stretched thin
With stretch marks
And faded scars
Freckles
The color of old blanket chests
I have folded up myself
And put her inside the chest Wrapped in old hand stitched quilts
Sterling silver baby spoons Marriage certificates
Old stained linen napkins
I fold myself up
Like a fitted sheet
But I don't know how to fold
A goddamn fitted sheet
Nor do I know
How to do THIS
I catch my reflection
In grocery stores
As I take food out of my Mom's cart Placing them on random shelves I look cheerful enough
Rugosa rose lips
Summer popsicle hair
I smile
I laugh
But
But
Pine boxes
Of heirlooms
Books
Photography
Poetry
Broken dolls
And me
Wound up
In a knot
Turkey vultures
Circle
In the foggy
June sky.

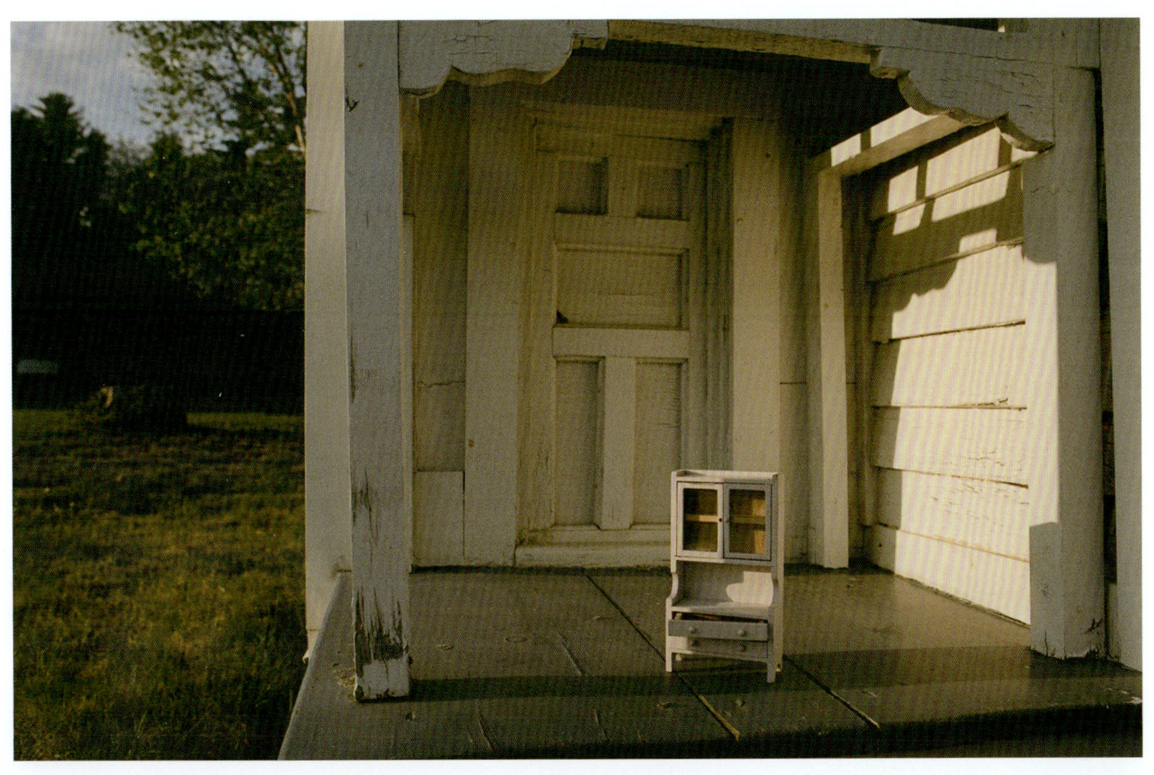

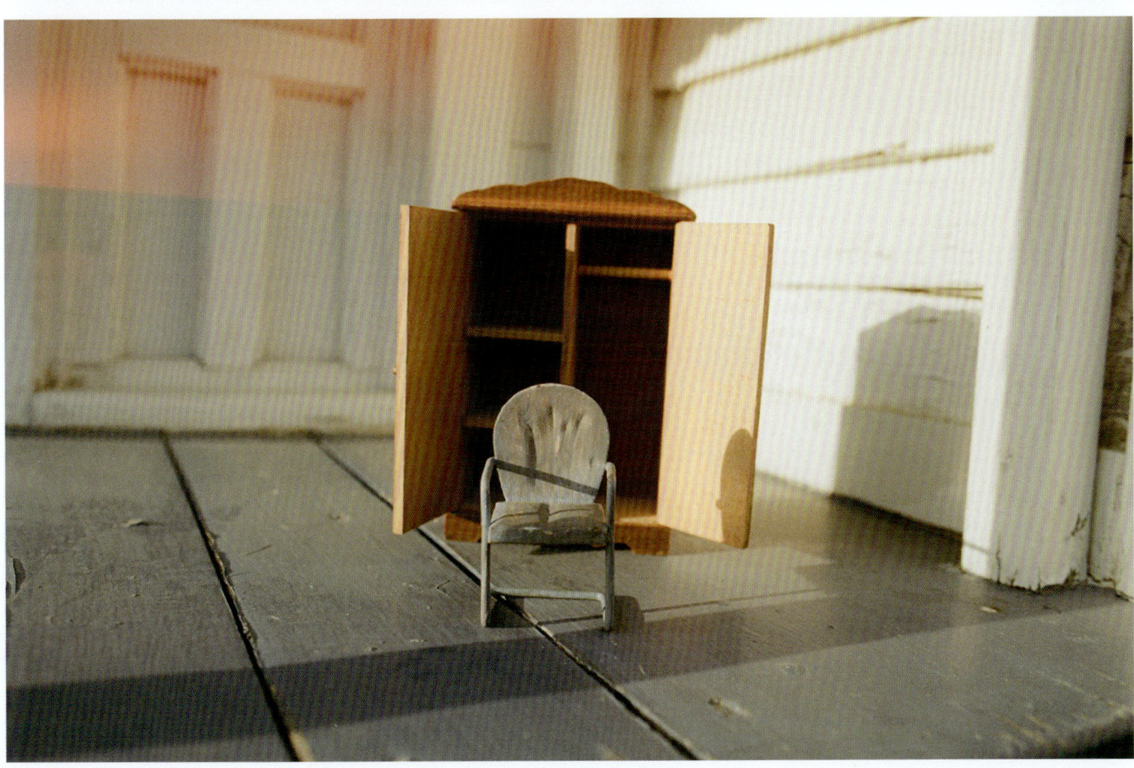

Turkey vultures
Circle
In the foggy
June sky.

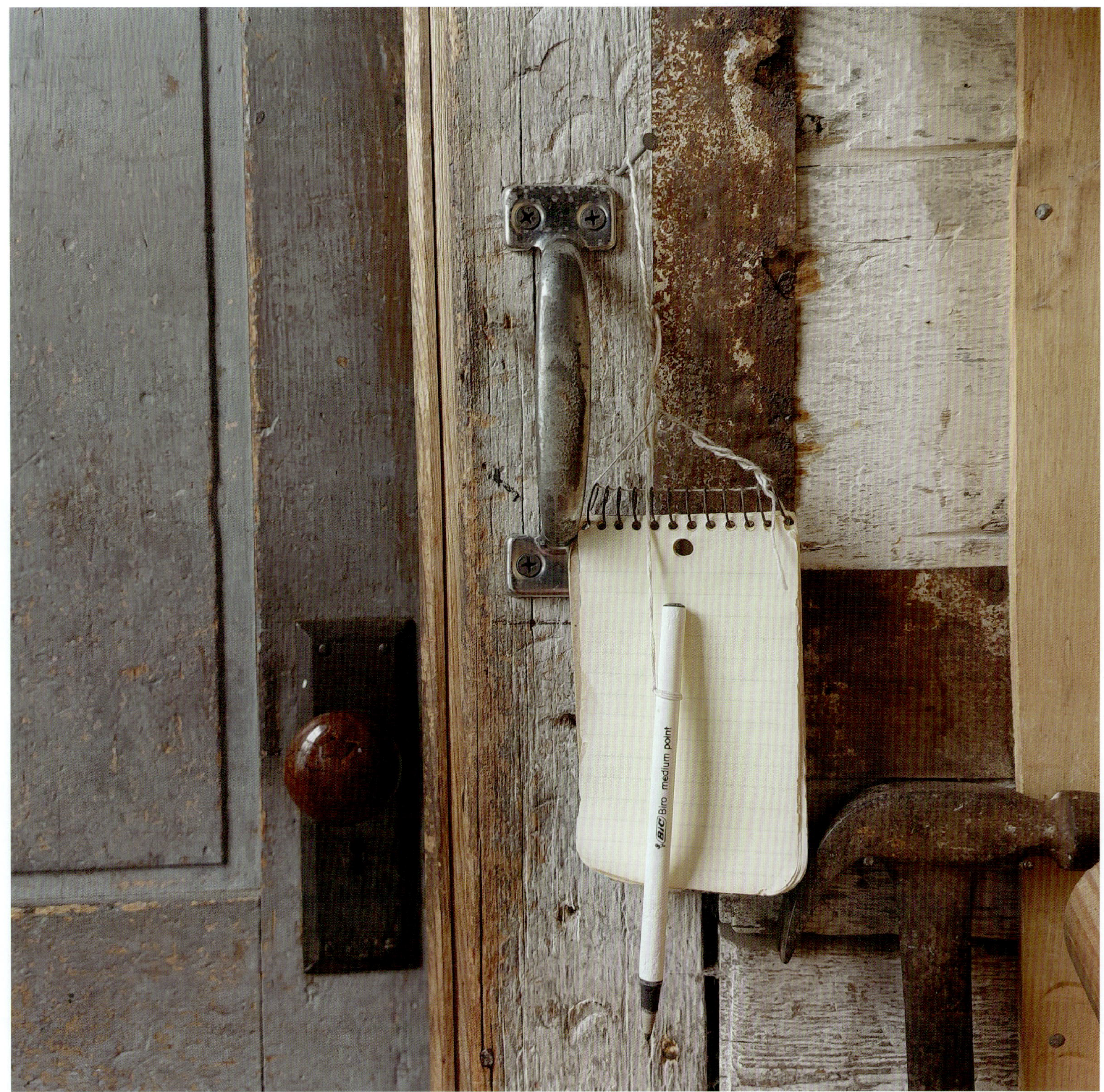
BIC Biro medium point

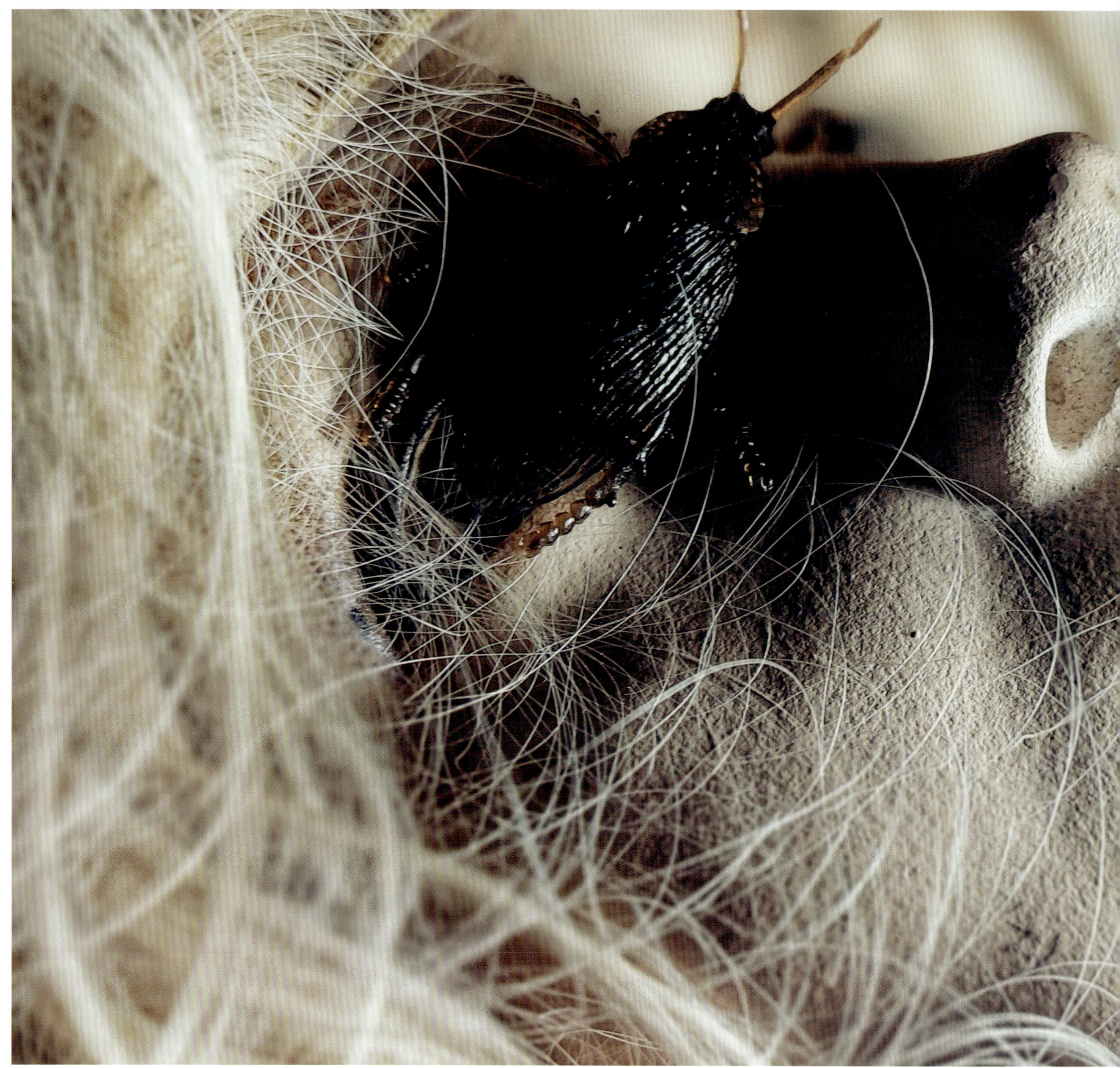

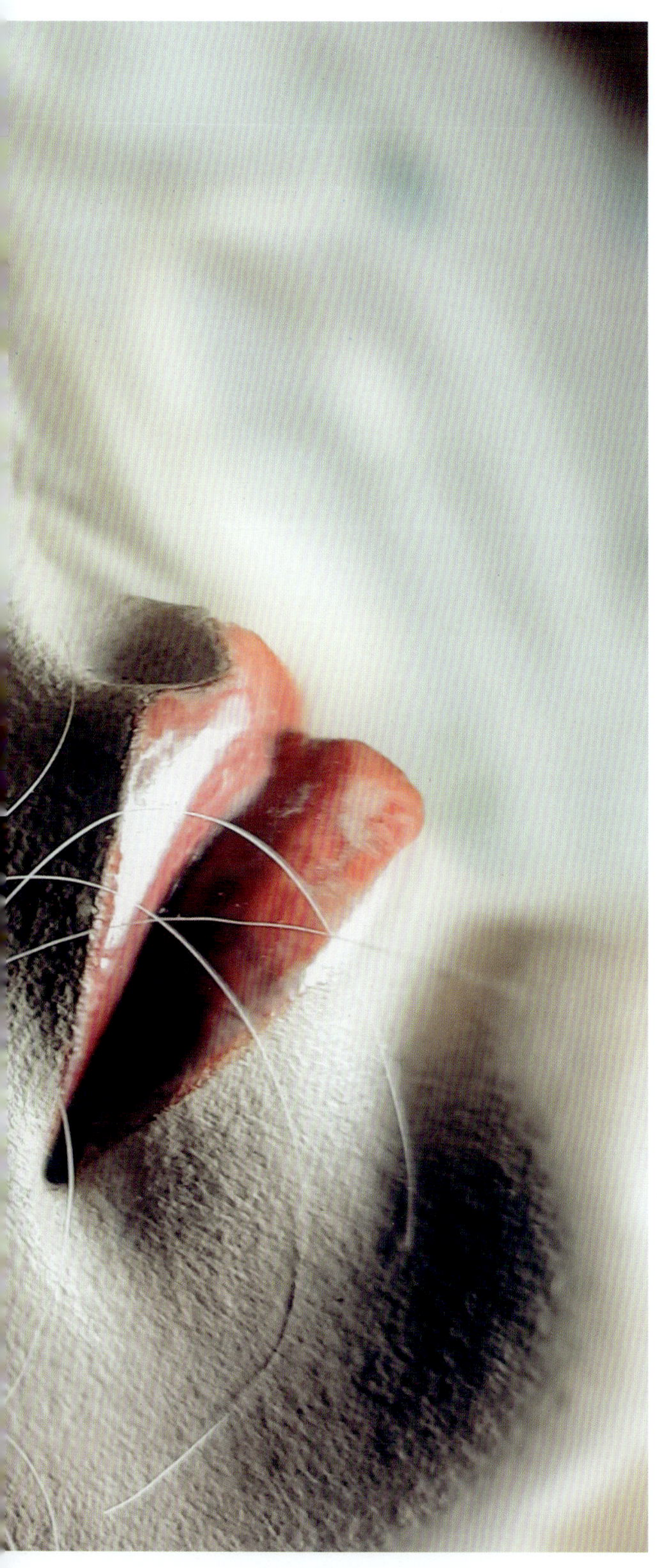

I catch my reflection
In windows
Of shops
Of old houses
With Squirrels living
in their walls
I see this woman
With a face made of
birch bark.

I would like to thank the following for love, support, laughter, everything:
My Ma, Ed, Carrie, Spencer, Queene, the ocean, Amy, Patti, Adam, Rhonda, Ronald, Fe, Craig, Kate C., Anne, punk rock, jazz, WERU, seals, my father, my Nana, Henry Rollins, Ian MacKaye, John Coltrane, every cat I have ever had, every cow I have ever kissed, and many more. Thank you.

Kristie began taking photographs with an old digital Nikon. She fell in love with film and proceeded to buy a Nikkormat. The cameras used in this book are:
Nikon D3000, Nikkormat, Pentax K1000, Rolleicord, various Mamiyas, and perhaps an Olympus film camera. She has begun a collection of various cameras. Her favorite is still the 35mm Nikkormat.